LEITH AT RANDOM

LEITH AT RANDOM

DAVID STEWART VALENTINE

Published by Porthole Publications
143 East Trinity Road
Edinburgh EH5 3PP

© DAVID STEWART VALENTINE 2006

first printed 2004
new edition 2005
reprinted 2006, 2007

A CIP Record for this book is available from the
British Cataloguing in Publication Data Office.

ISBN 0-9548642-0-4

Cover Illustration: 'Leith at Random' reproduced by
courtesy of South Leith Parish Church, Leith

Printed by Thomson Litho, East Kilbride, Glasgow
Design and Layout by Priority Graphic Design, Edinburgh

LEITH AT RANDOM

DAVID STEWART VALENTINE

Published by Porthole Publications
143 East Trinity Road
Edinburgh EH5 3PP

FOREWORD

The first written reference to Leith dates from the twelfth century and over the Centuries since then, many books and articles have told the story of the development of Leith from a small fishing village to becoming one of the Country's most important sea ports.

During the last 50 years, Leith has seen many changes as much of its industry, including the port, went into decline. But, despite these difficult times, Leith's people lived up to their motto "Persevere", and today we see a new Leith full of modern development in housing, retail stores and commercial activities.

Whilst there are times we can all yearn for what is often described as "the good old days", we must look at the future with optimism. David Valentine has written about a number of changes and happenings in Leith during the 20th Century, and his publication "Leith at Random" is a record of that time. It is an enjoyable read and will keep Leithers at home and abroad in touch with their roots.

I hope that in the years ahead, the people of Leith will continue to nurture that "community spirit" that I and those of my generation and generations before me enjoyed, and they will have the same pride that I have when I am asked during my travels, "where do you come from?" and I say with great pride and affection............"I am a Leither".

Sir Tom Farmer, CBE., KCSG.

ACKNOWLEDGEMENTS

Grateful acknowledgement is made to Jean Dick for the preparation of the manuscripts, to Dave Cormie for carrying out the unenviable task of proof reading and to Eddie Prior, a fellow Leither, for the book design.

My special thanks go to Walter Taylor for permitting me to use his collection of photographs and to Edinburgh City Libraries for their services. The help and support given to me by my wife Irene was also appreciated.

Lastly, this book would not have been published without the encouragement and support of Gerald Farmer, and I am grateful to him for providing this opportunity to bring Leith at Random to you.

David Valentine 2006

PREFACE

As a boy, I was brought up just a stone's throw from the Foot of Leith Walk, and have always had an inner sense that Leith was somehow different from the stuffy refinement of the City, with its financial institutions, university, fine buildings, shops and streets. The centre of my small world at that time was enclosed by the busy railway station, tramcars, horses and carts, family shops, the Links, and by the friendly people that you would meet in the Kirkgate who would smile and often stop you for a chat.

The Gretna disaster in 1915 was still spoken of as if it was only yesterday, and there were few in Leith who did not believe that the community was hoodwinked into the amalgamation with Edinburgh in 1920, indeed, many people still do! Leithers were different - they lived by the sea and drew their strength from the sharp east winds and salt air, which over the centuries had hardened them into a strong community. 'Sunny Leith' was not a compliment to the weather, but had more to do with the strong demeanour of its people who have had to smile through some very rough times over the centuries since it was no more than a hamlet at the mouth of a small river. Thankfully, the town has survived invasion, burning, siege, plague and the attentions of the City on the skyline, but another crisis now faces the community as it tries to adapt to the new developments which are threatening to engulf its historic past.

What would Queen Victoria have thought about it now I wonder, as she gazes from her stony pedestal at the Foot of Leith Walk? For me, the memories have mellowed since those days in the thirties, but I still breathe in the salt air whenever I can, and wander around the streets like many others searching for the ghosts of a bygone age.

The sadness of these thoughts which had germinated between the wars was that Leith had begun to lose its self respect, and even its once proud motto 'Persevere' had a hollow ring to it. The community had become dispirited, and no one seemed to care, until the late 1970s, when years of pleading for action finally began to bear fruit. Today's developments may not be to everyone's taste, but it is to the future that Leith must now look, as it has much to offer.

Since the publication of *Leith at Random* in 2004, plans for the future of Leith have been announced by Forth Ports plc. which will see major changes made to the Port of Leith, Western Harbour and Granton Harbour under the heading of Edinburgh Forthside. This two mile stretch of shoreline will become the centre of Edinburgh's Waterfront City, and over a twenty year programme will be seen as the *largest single planned development area in the history of Edinburgh*.

The old town of Leith is now at the crossroads and the regeneration of the community, old and new, is vital for the long term future, otherwise it may be left to wither and die.

David Valentine 2006

CONTENTS

THE PORT OF QUEENS

Now that the former Royal Yacht Britannia is permanently berthed alongside the Ocean Terminal, it is interesting to look back over the centuries to remind ourselves that Leith was once referred to as The Port of Queens.

In 1423/24, after the marriage of James I of Scotland to Joan of Beaufort, the daughter of the Earl of Somerset, they landed at Leith from Berwick to a rousing welcome. In 1437, after the assassination of James I at Perth, the young James II, who had secretly been conveyed to Stirling via Leith, again visited the town but this time to welcome the arrival of Mary of Gueldres whom he had married by proxy in Brussels. James II was killed at the Siege of Roxburgh Castle, and was succeeded by James III, who married Margaret the daughter of King Christian of Denmark who came to marry him at Holyrood. The next visit of a Queen to Leith was during the reign of James V, who was known as 'The Poor Man's King.' He pursued Mary daughter of the Duke of Vendome for some time, but he had his heart set on Madelaine de Valois, daughter of King Francis I of France. The Royal couple were married in 1537, and Madelaine was said to have kissed the ground on The Shore, and thanked God that she and her husband had come safely over the sea. Sadly, she died of tuberculosis some months later.

A view of the Shore, Leith, 1693

A Royal resident in Leith was the Queen Mother, Mary of Lorraine, who had been proclaimed Regent and had conveyed the Town into a Burgh of Barony and promised that at some time it would be erected into a Royal Burgh. The Queen Mother died before this promise was carried through. In August 1561, Mary, Queen of Scots landed at Leith from France and was said to have stayed briefly at Andrew Lamb's house before proceeding to the Palace of Holyroodhouse. After her execution, Mary was succeeded by her son James who became James VI of Scotland and also James I of England. He married Princess Anne of Denmark by proxy in 1589, and the Royal couple landed at Leith in 1590. They were said to have stayed for several days in the King's Wark before proceeding to the Palace of Holyroodhouse where the Coronation took place.

It was another two hundred and fifty years before another Queen was to grace the shores of Leith, when in 1842 Queen Victoria landed at Granton, where she and Prince Albert received a memorable welcome, and visited Leith the following day. Other visits to Leith have been made by Queen Alexandra who came from Denmark, and the much loved Queen Mary. The Queen Mother visited Trinity House and also opened Lamb's House Day Centre, and our present Queen has made several visits to Leith, some on board her Royal Yacht Britannia.

COAT OF ARMS

There have been several variations of the Leith Coat of Arms, but the original depicts a woman and child, seated in a ship over which is spread a canopy surmounted by a turret pierced with four small apertures, and upon the tutela, or shrine, a ball and cross is placed. Two loop holed towers, each bearing a simple cross, rise up on either side, almost to the height of the central projection. Both of these are surmounted by pillars elevated from the foot of the canopy. The ship has a high peaked prow and

The Arms of Leith, 1563

poop, and carries two masts with furled sails, and two pennants in the breeze. The seal from which this design is taken dates from 1563. It was probably the intention of the Leith Coat of Arms to convey a representation of the Madonna and infant Saviour, the cross standing over the ball signifying that spiritual power is above the temporal, and the ship carrying its cargo representing the Town's maritime and sacred past.

A GRAND NIGHT OUT

The evening of Sunday 11 October 1998 was to become a memorable one for Leith as it signalled the inaugural reception aboard the former Royal Yacht Britannia, now berthed in the Western Harbour. The guests were drawn mainly from the community in Leith in recognition of their services to the area, and the event was hosted by Sir Tom and Lady Farmer.

The evening was fine but cold, and the guests assembled in the Visitor Centre,

The Former Royal Yacht Britannia : Being fitted out before moving to a permanent berth alongside the Ocean Terminal

where, after checking in, you could study plans and displays telling all about Britannia, inspect the Royal launch berthed in its own small dock, and sip a little champagne to help you on your way. One of the most interesting exhibits on display was the beautifully preserved binnacle from the Royal George, the last sailing Royal Yacht which brought George IV to Leith in 1822, and where a commemorative plaque marking this event can be seen on The Shore. When the guests went on board, one realised how small the vessel was, but yet she had managed to travel over one million miles, and undertake around one thousand official visits since her launch from Clydebank in 1953. The buffet supper consumed, and the tour around the yacht completed, it was time to go on deck to listen to a selection of music played from the quayside by the Lowland Band of the Scottish Division, followed by the Pipes and Drums of the 1st Battalion, the Argyll and Sutherland Highlanders, who beat Retreat. The guests then mustered on the starboard side for the grand fireworks finale which lit up the sky, and cast ghostly shadows from across the waters where Henry Robb's shipyard once stood, and where the heart of the working community of Leith once beat.

All too quickly it seemed, the evening was over, and everyone came away asking themselves if this was really the beginning of the new Leith, and although there were many regrets about the passing of the old, these thoughts were tempered by the prospect of this new Leith which was now beginning to dawn.

NAUTICAL COLLEGE

The first Navigation School in Leith was opened in 1855 in a room belonging to the Mariners' Church in Commercial Street which got off to an encouraging start until its Master, John Newton, a Londoner, left to take up a position with Glasgow Navigation School. His successor, who did not have the necessary qualifications, failed to build on previous success, and soon there were only three boys left.

The Board of Trade wanted to close the School altogether at this point, but a young man named James Bolam, who came from Newcastle, was chosen as the new Master. He took up his position in January 1861, and soon enrolled sufficient pupils to be able to appoint an assistant. The School moved from the Mariners' Church to the Tolbooth Wynd, but later returned to the Church before moving into a converted warehouse in Dock Place in 1882. Bolam had continual problems with the Board of Trade, and from time to time he and his assistant suffered great hardship due to the rules which were being placed upon them.

A Science and Art School was also being run by Bolam from Cromwell House in Great Junction Street, but his dream was to have a new purpose built college for the Port. Three years after the move to Dock Place, the Balfour Commission set up an investigation into educational endowments made before 1872, and Bolam and the Managers of Leith Navigation School, together with Leith School Board and Leith Science School, fought to keep all funds in Leith, and eventually financial assistance was secured for nautical training. In 1887 a building fund was opened, and Bolam's constant lobbying for support and funds eventually led to a sum of £4,000 being raised, and the search began for a suitable site. The Sailors' Home and Leith High School sites were both considered as suitable locations, but an application made to the Commissioners of the Harbour and Docks for Leith for a site near to the Dock Offices was turned down. However, the Commissioners did offer a site in Commercial Street, and during 1901/02, Scotland's first purpose built nautical college was completed.

The new college was designed by William Laidlaw in the English Baroque style, and in honour of its new status, the School was renamed Leith Nautical College. It was opened on 4 February 1903 by Lord Balfour of Burleigh, the Secretary of State. The site was not ideal, however, and the basement was subject to periodic flooding, and once, in 1907, the building was invaded by rats from the adjoining railway stables. At this stage, James Bolam was sixty-four years old, but he was to remain as Principal for a further twenty years.

The College was given Central Institution status in 1903, and this gave opportunities for improved funding. Wireless telegraphy classes commenced in 1913, when thirteen students enrolled for the Postmaster General's Certificate, and in 1923, arrangements were made with Heriot Watt College for access to their laboratories due to the inadequate facilities then available within their own building.

On 31 December 1923, James Bolam retired, having given sixty-three years service to the College, but he was still able to attend the opening of the new laboratory building in 1927, when it was opened by Lord Novar. James died at the age of ninety-one, two months before the College was further extended, and some fifty years later, his College moved to a showpiece building in Milton Road. Sadly, within ten years of the move, it was closed down after it had been created as one of the finest colleges in the country.

THE GREAT MICHAEL

At the small harbour of Newhaven the famous warship of James IV, the *Great Michael*, was built and launched in 1511, and was said to have been the largest vessel at that time to have floated on the sea. Jacques Tarette was the builder, or naval architect, and he certainly went out of his way to create the most magnificent ship in the world, much to the envy of the King of Scotland, Francis I and Henry VIII. This extraordinary vessel is said to have been compared in history with the *Bishop's Barge*, built in the previous reign by Kennedy, Bishop of St. Andrews, but this was purely a merchant vessel, and was wrecked and pillaged on the coast of England around 1474.

Some claimed that the *Great Michael* was the first armour-clad vessel, as amidships her sides were padded with solid oak, ten feet thick. She had cost some £30,000 to build, which was an enormous sum of money in those days, but James IV had planned to sail her to the Mediterranean with a Scottish fleet in order to visit Jerusalem.

The Great Michael : The famous warship of George IV built and launched at Newhaven in 1511

This huge vessel required so much timber that she was said to have consumed all of the oak wood in Fife and Norway. She was 240 feet long and 36 feet wide. Armed with many heavy guns, she was capable of carrying 300 mariners, 120 cannoniers and 1,000 soldiers, together with her captains and quartermasters. Sir Andrew Wood was commander of the ship and Robert Barton the master skipper.

In April 1514, the *Great Michael* was sold to Louis XII by the Duke of Albany in the name of the Scottish government, but this once great ship was left to rot in the harbour at Brest in north-west France.

A LITTLE PIECE OF NORWAY

To the passer by, the former Scandinavian Lutheran Church in North Junction Street may not even merit a second glance, but it does remind us of the time when Leith, as an important seaport, was host to seamen from many parts of the world.

It was in 1863 that Johan Cordt Harmens Storjohan, a graduate in Divinity, arrived in Edinburgh from Bergen in order to study the history of the Church in Scotland, and he became concerned when he discovered that seamen from Scandinavia had no place to worship. He committed himself to establishing a Norwegian Church in Leith, and in 1864 a committee was formed under the title 'The Scandinavian Seamen's Mission for Leith and other ports in the Firth of Forth.'

The Committee managed to raise the sum of £100 to pay for the first year's salary of a pastor and promised to give continued support should the Mission be successful. In 1865, Adrias Michael Hansen came to Leith as the first pastor, and among those who welcomed him was Christian Salvesen, founder of the Salvesen Company. Four years later a new church was built in North Junction Street by James Simpson, a Leith Architect, who adapted a design by Johan Schroder of Copenhagen. The church was officially opened by Pastor Storjohan, and the following day, a special service was conducted by Pastor J Urain and the Rev. Norman Salvesen, MA BD, who was at that time pastor to the Mission. Pastors from other Norwegian churches in Scotland also attended, as well as Dr Nils Hjelmveit, the Norwegian Minister of Churches and the Norwegian Ambassador, Erik Colban.

When you next pass by the former church, stop and look for the boulder which bears an inscription in Norwegian which says that this boulder was brought to Leith by a ship which had run aground, but which had later been refloated. When the ship docked in Leith, the boulder was found embedded in the bottom of the bow section, and later found a resting place at the Church door.

Despite some war damage to the building in 1941, King Haakon and Crown Prince Olaf attended the 75th Anniversary of the Norwegian Seamen's Churches in October 1943.

Today, the former church building is home to the Leith School of Art which was founded by Mark and Charlotte Cheverton who were both tragically killed in a road accident in 1991. The School, however, has continued to develop their tradition for teaching, and it is now fully recognised by the major art institutions in Scotland.

TOM THUMB

This story concerns a tiny Eskimo who was brought back to Leith by the master of a whaler at the beginning of the nineteenth century. He came from the Davis Straits, and when the whaler arrived in Leith, crowds flocked to the quayside to see him, and prevented the unloading of the vessel. The Master found it necessary to send the little Eskimo into lodgings ashore, but the crowds still flocked to see him and his canoe which weighed only sixteen pounds. They showed great interest in his clothes, blow darts and the other articles which he had brought with him. He was so popular that the Master decided to exhibit him in a nearby warehouse, and from the admission money he bought Tom Thumb more suitable clothes.

His popularity continued, and an exhibition of the little man's skills was arranged. This took the form of a race to Inchkeith and back, with his little canoe competing against a six oared whale boat. His skilful use of the single paddle left the whale boat far behind, and he occasionally stopped to let them catch up. When they did, he would turn over in the water and right himself as if to mock the opposing oarsmen, and easily won the race.

The crowd loved this, and the race was run again, but this time the little Eskimo also used his blowpipe to target ship's biscuits floating on the water. All the vantage points were lined with spectators who cheered and waved to him, and the water was crowded with small boats almost as far as the Martello Tower.

THE LEITH POLICE DISMISSETH US

The date of the formation of a Police force in Leith is not accurately known, but the Edinburgh City Police was formed in 1805, and it seems likely that the Leith force was formed by the Second Police Act of 1806. Prior to that, an Act of 1771 made provision for the election of thirty Police Commissioners, but they were concerned not with crime but with the welfare of the community, where water supply, sanitation and lighting posed major problems for the town.

In 1798, a booklet was printed which contained instructions by the Magistrates of Leith to be observed by the constables in discharge of their duty. The Commissioners of Leith at that time were appointed by the Lord Provost and Magistrates of the City of Edinburgh, and when a further Act was passed in 1827 this enabled Commissioners in Leith to extend their responsibility for the administration of Justice, and for the regulation of the Police.

The Commissioners were also authorised to provide a Court House, and this led to the building of a new Police Station in Constitution Street which is still in use today.

Until 1848, Leith had two separate and distinct public bodies - the Police Commissioners and the Town Council, although certain members managed to be elected to both of these. Leith was in the fortunate position of having offices in the Tolbooth Wynd in addition to the new Police headquarters in Queen Charlotte Street. The Act of 1848 clarified the existing position, and this resulted in the Town Council becoming Commissioners for the administration of the law, and the Council offices in the Tolbooth Wynd were sold when the administration moved into the new building.

Leith Police Badge

With the amalgamation of Leith with Edinburgh in 1920, the Leith Burgh Police ceased to exist and was merged into the ranks of Edinburgh City Police. Leith became 'D' Division, but had always been referred to as 'Leith' because of its historical connections. The Division still operates from the same building in Queen Charlotte Street which was built in 1827.

SERVICE BEFORE SELF

One of Leith's well known police personalities was Willie Merrilees who was born in a top flat off the Kirkgate, and later lived with his family in a two roomed flat in St. Andrew's Street. By his own admission, he was no scholar, but he had a very eventful childhood, and was very much influenced by the Sunday School which he attended at the Mission in St Andrew's Hall. He worked as a driller during the First World War, and there are many stories told of his rescues of people from drowning in the docks. He married in 1919, and lived in a small house in Bridge Street, but times were very hard after the war, and luck was with him when he managed to become a plain clothes officer in Edinburgh. He was only 5'6" tall, had a basic education, and had lost the fingers of his left hand, and he could only guess at his future prospects at that time. He did not take long to make an impression as a plain clothes officer, however, and in 1926 he was promoted to the rank of Sergeant in charge of Recruiting and Licensing. Four years later he was appointed Detective Inspector. In 1940

"I'm Willie Merrilees - policeman" :
Disguised as a railway porter at the arrest of Werner Walti

he became a Detective Superintendent in charge of the CID, and was awarded the King's Police Medal in 1944. He became Detective Chief Superintendent in 1947, was appointed Chief Constable of the Lothians and Peebles Constabulary in 1950, and received the OBE in 1959.

The stories of Willie Merrilees and his crackdown on vice, drugs and even spies are legend, and he became known for his part in the Kosmo Club case which exposed the shady dealings of Edinburgh night life. He also took part in the arrest of the spy Werner Walti at Waverley Station, when in 1940, Willie, disguised as a porter, disarmed and arrested Walti, who was later hanged at Wandsworth Prison.

Willie died some years ago, but he was a good friend to the community of Leith, and when introduced more formally he was always proud to say, "I'm Willie Merrilees - policeman."

A GRAVEN IMAGE

For many years a block of stone lay on the sands at Leith which, it was reported, was intended to be used to create a statue to honour Oliver Cromwell, the Lord High Protector. The magistrates of the City of Edinburgh had ordered the stone, but within a few days of placing it on the sands, news came of the death of Cromwell and the idea was abandoned.

The stone lay on the sands until 1788, when it was removed by Mr. Walter Ross who erected it on the sloping ground at Ann Street. It stood around eight feet in height, and had been shaped into a rough human form by workmen at a local quarry. After the death of Mr. Ross, the crudely shaped stone found a new owner, and it was re-erected near to the spot where it had previously been positioned. There was much pressure exerted to have the unwanted figure removed, and it was eventually taken to the Water of Leith where it was broken up.

GREAT JUNCTION STREET

Great Junction Street is not the most beautiful street in the world, but even in its drabness it does have a place in the historic past of Leith. Once it was commonly known as Junction Road, but there is no evidence to suggest that there has ever been a Leith street of this name.

The junction came about when South Leith and North Leith were joined by Junction Bridge which was built in 1818, but even then there was some confusion over what to call it. At first it was called South Junction Street which led to North Junction Street, and then the whole length from the Foot of Leith Walk to Portland Place was named Great Junction Street, but finally the present division between Great and North Junction Streets was made, and the names have remained unchanged ever since. There was also a Junction Place at one time, which local people called Firebrigade Street because of the Fire Station which was opened there in 1878.

Great Junction Street followed the line of the ramparts which were built by the French before the Siege of Leith, and the rough, open ground which later followed that line was eventually laid with 'causie setts' in 1864, although the

Great Junction Street : A view from the former State Cinema corner to the Foot of Leith Walk

level of the surface was set too high for the laying of the tram lines in 1871, and the whole surface had to be relevelled and relaid. For over two hundred years, the road was likened to an unmade country track, and as far back as 1822, maps still showed it to be only a proposed road. The first building of any note to be built in Great Junction Street was St Thomas' Church, built in classical style to a design by William Bell between 1824/25. This was followed some sixteen years later when Dr Bell's School was built to a design by RR Dickson and completed in 1839. Apart from these two buildings, much of the ground at that time was still open, and was used mainly as builders' yards and storage.

It was really the growth of North Leith which began to make Great Junction Street an important thoroughfare, as the increasing pressure of traffic on the narrow Leith streets began to cause many problems. The construction of Leith Walk led to the building of Constitution Street, which relieved some of these pressures, and the new Great Junction Street began to take much of the traffic from North Leith which had previously followed the historic route through Coburg Street and Bridge Street.

The names of many of the streets leading off Great Junction Street are interesting. Henderson Street for instance, was named after Dr John Henderson, who was Provost of Leith from 1875 to 1884. He was responsible for the Leith Improvement Scheme which began in 1881, and which disposed of many of the wynds and closes which threaded their way through the area. Pirrie Street was probably named after David Pirrie, who was a wright, who had a workshop in St Anthony Street and also owned a house in Great Junction Street opposite the street which now bears his name.

Bonnington Road was part of a new route formed between Leith and Canonmills, and is mentioned in a charter for Stewartfield dated 1735. The point where Bonnington Road joins Great Junction Street was once known as the Bonny Town Port which was an opening in the old Siege wall. Bangor Road was known as the road which led to a local slateworks, and probably got its name from Bangor in North Wales, a major slate quarrying area. Bowling Green Street was built over the site of an eighteenth century bowling green, and has now largely been superseded by streets around The Quilts, which was said to have been located where a game resembling skittles was once played. King Street is listed as far back as 1773 but who was the King? Some say it was probably George III.

Taylor Gardens, situated in front of the former Leith Hospital was named after William Taylor, who was once the Chairman of the Parish Council. It was once the site of the Leith Poorhouse which was later relocated at the Eastern General Hospital. Despite several references to Ballantyne Road being named after Robert Ballantyne, Abbot of Holyrood, it is more likely that it was named after the builders, Grieve Ballantyne who built there in 1896. Mill Lane is referred to as far back as 1693, and refers to its association with the mills which operated above Junction Bridge. The final reference is made to Cable's Wynd which is named after Henry Capell, who was a brewer in Leith, and made a free maltster in 1660. The name is probably Dutch or Flemish in origin.

A DAMP SQUIB

An incident is recorded when, in February 1940, a trawler strayed out of the safe channel in the Forth just off Inchkeith, and was in danger of striking a mine. The gun battery on Inchkeith attempted to warn the trawler, and fired a six inch practice shell across her bows to warn her of the danger. The trawler took the appropriate action, but the round ricocheted off the surface of the water, passed through the walls of the old Neptune Mills, destroyed an air raid shelter and some garden huts, and eventually ended up in the sitting room of a tenement flat in Salamander Street, destroying the contents. Remarkably, the occupant received only minor cuts and shock, and the shell is reported to have been returned to Inchkeith with best wishes.

SEAFIELD BATHS

It may be difficult to believe that Leith was once known for its fine beaches and bathing facilities, and also for Seafield Baths which stood at the east end of Leith Links. Designed by John Paterson, and built in 1810/13, seventeen plunge baths and a swimming pool were provided there at a cost of £8,000. The money was raised by shareholders who each subscribed £50 towards the cost, and acquired the right to the use of the baths in perpetuity.

Before the building of these baths, sea bathing had become very popular, but no facilities were then available for changing. In order to accommodate those intending to bathe in the sea, a small timber framed cabin on wheels, with horse and servants could be hired on application to James Morton, who could be found at the Royal Oak, near to the Glass House in Salamander Street. These bathing houses were advertised in the Edinburgh Courant of May 1761, and may have been the first in Scotland.

HISTORIC HOUSES

The Improvement Scheme which was adopted by Leith Councillors in 1880 had the effect of removing several buildings which were of historic interest. The area involved in the scheme was one of the oldest in Leith, and over the centuries witnessed much of the turbulent times which had been caused by the granting of the harbour and mills of Leith to Edinburgh by Robert the Bruce in 1329. Sir Robert Logan of Restalrig also sold off parts of the banks and harbour to the city, and restricted access to a very narrow and inconvenient lane to the North of the Tolbooth Wynd. The area exposed for development included the Old Tolbooth, the Council Chamber of Lennox, Parliament Square, and then to the south, St Anthony's preceptory, and all the adjacent buildings, including the old Grammar School. A strange-looking building facing onto the harbour at Coalhill was occupied as a public house, and there were several other buildings adjoining which were in a poor state of repair. There was some hope at the time that local antiquarians might rescue the old building as there were a number of opinions as to its former use. It is recorded that shortly after the murder of the Regent Murray, a headquarter was established in Leith, and Lennox used the building as his Council Chamber. A sculptured stone once adorned the building, and the Council Chamber, although somewhat neglected, was considered to be a most handsome and spacious chamber which had been erected by Mary of Lorraine for the meetings of her Council during the time of the regency.

Mary's name again appears in connection with the construction of the Old Tolbooth, which was also affected by the Improvement Scheme. A plaque had been placed in front of the building bearing the Royal arms, with the date 1565, and the initials M R, and the motto 'In defens.' This building was demolished in 1819, but the sculptured stone was retained and can now be seen in South Leith Church.

The district of St Anthony was directly affected by building development, and in 1614, King James VI granted the charter for King James' Hospital, which stood on the south side of the Kirkgate in an area then called the New Tombs. There is also evidence to suggest that the property between Merrylees Court, St Anthony's Lane and the Port in the Kirkgate was held by the Knights Templar, and a number of skeletons were found in St Anthony's Lane, all in an advanced state of decay.

There were several other buildings of note, including the Citadel, where the first newspaper in Scotland is said to have been printed; Trinity House, founded in 1555, containing many fine paintings; the mansion of Lord Balmerino, where Charles II stayed when he paid a visit to his troops on Leith Links; and a rather strange building which once stood in Queen Street, and which bore the date 1516, which was used as an Episcopal chapel. The Sheriff Brae too was of much interest, and was closely linked with the Gladstone family. The first directory of Leith, which was published by a man called Williamson, contains the name of a Captain Aire whose name occurred in a song about smuggling and John Logan, of Constitution Hill who was a minister.

BELIEVE IT OR NOT !

Many years ago, a shoemaker in the Kirkgate had a night out with some of his friends in one of the local taverns. After a few ales, he began to make his way home to the Yardheads, and as he passed through St Anthony's Lane he was confronted by what appeared to be a mort cloth standing on end, and without any apparent means of support. He was, as he said, "no afraid o' twa yairds o' velvet," but as he proceeded on his way, he was engulfed by the garment. He was blinded, breathless, and now quite frightened, but as he threw off the wrap which had held him, he was astonished to be confronted by 'a beautiful angel.' He did not delay any further, but took to his heels and fled home as quickly as he could.

The Green Lady, sometimes referred to as Green Jenny was no angel however, as it turned out that her husband, a local brewer, had been declared bankrupt, and she had managed to salvage the company from his creditors. She watched over her brewery by night and day in order to prevent intruders, and dressed in her green velvet cloak she would signal to her workmen with her white apron underneath when any suspicious character was seen in the lane so that steps could be taken to investigate. A very human ghost indeed !

FIGHT GAME

The Leith Victoria Amateur Athletic Club was formed by workers from Henry Robb's Shipyard, and occupied an old wooden army hut at the Marine Parade, which had been vacated by the Leith Swimming Club. Boxing soon became the main interest, and Tancy Lee became principal instructor to the club, which is thought to be the second oldest boxing club in Great Britain, with only Battersea Boys' Club having been formed at an earlier date.

Many fine boxers have emerged from the sweaty rooms of the boxing club, and names like Alec Ireland and George Mackenzie, Alec Bell and Manuel 'Kid' Abrew, and many others will still be recalled in bars around Leith. It was not only the men who wore the gloves that brought Leith to the forefront of boxing, but the name Nat Dresner, who became synonymous with the promotion of the sport during the 1920's. He was able to attract large crowds to his big fights in Edinburgh, but his health became a problem, and he died at his home in James Place, overlooking Leith Links in 1928, at the age of 46. Nat had put so much effort into the sport , that on his death, boxing in the east was never the same again, and Glasgow soon became the recognised home of the Scottish professional game.

It comes as no great surprise to find that Leith was also to produce two world class boxing referees, one a Leith man called George Smith, and the other a Musselburgh man called Eugene Henderson, who both earned their boxing spurs with Leith Victoria Boxing Club. Eugene handled several world title fights, including Peter Kane versus Jackie Jurich, Freddie Mills against Gus Lesnevich, and the Randolph Turpin versus Sugar Ray Robinson fight. George Smith became the first Scotsman to referee a World Heavyweight Title Fight when, in 1966, Muhammad Ali beat Henry Cooper. He also refereed the great boxers of his day, including Ken Buchanan versus Jim Watt, Walter McGowan against Jackie Brown and also Chic Calderwood against John 'Cowboy' McCormack.

Leith has had a long history of being able to produce the best of boxing skills, whether it be in the ranks of amateur or professional, and the members of Leith Victoria Boxing Club have managed to keep the name of Leith to the forefront.

THE KOBENHAVN

The Leith shipyard of Ramage & Ferguson built 296 vessels of various types during the 56 years of the yard's existence, and was noted for good design and workmanship. Among the most famous sailing ships built was the *Kobenhavn*, one of the largest to be built in a British yard. She was commissioned by the East Asiatic Company of Denmark after the end of the First World War, and was used by the Danish navy as a training ship. Baron Juel Brockdorff of the Danish Royal Navy supervised the completion of the *Kobenhavn* while on the stocks in Leith, and during her stay in Copenhagen before her maiden voyage, she was visited by over 12,000 people, including the King and Queen of Denmark.

She had a deck length of 390 feet, a gross tonnage of 3,965 tons, and carried some 56,000sq.ft. of sail. Her figurehead, which was carved in Copenhagen out of teak, was a representation of Absalom, the nation's priest, who founded the Danish capital. On what proved to be her last voyage, and with Captain Andersen in command, the ship left Buenos Aires on December 14, 1928 with 15 officers and ratings and 45 cadets on board, but she became overdue, and after many searches was listed as missing with the closing entries made by Lloyds on January 1, 1930.

The Kobenhavn in full sail before being lost with all hands in 1928

Until the early years of the 20th century many ships still incorporated into their design remnants of the heavy decoration which had been a feature of full riggers in their heyday from the 16th century onwards.

The Kobenhavn had a distinctive 'gilt and gingerbread' decoration at her stern which gave her a very proud line.

A CHILLY RECEPTION

In 1903, Leith had the distinction of being the town where Sir Ernest Shackleton made his first appearance as a lecturer. At that time, he was Secretary to the Scottish Geographical Society in Edinburgh, and he came to the Assembly Rooms in Constitution Street to tell of his experiences with the National Antarctic Expedition of 1901, when he was a third lieutenant. Unfortunately, only twenty five people turned up, and in later years, Sir Ernest made light of his embarrassment at the low turnout which he said could have been accommodated around his dining room table.

To make matters worse, and in order to improve the attendance, Sir Ernest even invited his cabby inside, but he would have none of it, and even declined Sir Ernest's offer to pay someone to look after the horse while he was attending the lecture. Some years later, when Sir Ernest had gained distinction in South Polar exploration, he again visited Leith, but on that occasion the audience was large and enthusiastic.

MEETING HOUSE

Many years ago, the remains of a building once stood on the north side of the Yardheads between the streets we now call Cable's Wynd and King Street. It is said that the original building was built in 1688 by Alexander Mathieson, and was used as a Meeting-house by Leith Presbyterians when South Leith Church was under Episcopal domination. The Meeting-house was known as the Ark, and although the reason for this is not certain, it is recognised that the name is a reference to the Ark of the Covenant. The little road to the Ark was known as Mathieson's Wynd, and this followed the route of what we now know as Cable's Wynd. Four years after the opening of the Ark, the existing congregation, under their minister William Wishart took forcible possession of the parish church, and the Episcopalians became the Non-conformists. It then appears that the successors to the first congregation of the Ark were the Episcopalians who had themselves been ousted from the parish church. A South Leith session minute of 1709 notes that the Episcopalian Meeting-house in the Yardheads had been closed, as the minister was not properly qualified, but it seems that after a short lapse, services continued 'every Lord's day.'

The story of the Ark is not entirely clear, but tradition has it that John Wesley, the founder of Methodism may have preached at the Ark to a congregation which filled the hall, to the extent that people spilled onto the Meeting-house Green, and Wesley had to make his address from a window in the building. This was during a visit prior to 1764, and some years later, when the Ark had finally been abandoned as a place of worship, the building was used for other purposes. It was around 1775 that its time as a church came to an end, but many years later, local folk referred to it as 'John Knox's Church,' and told tales of the great reformer who had alas died over a century before the original Meeting-house was built !

THE DAY LEITH STOOD STILL

To many people, the name Gretna may conjure up an image of runaway couples and marriage ceremonies, but to Leithers the name still sends a chill down the spine, as it recalls that day in May 1915 when at Quintinshill, near Gretna, it was the scene of Britain's worst ever rail disaster.

The accident involved the officers and men of the 7th (Leith Volunteer) Battalion The Royal Scots, who were drawn mainly from the streets of Leith, with others from Musselburgh and other parts, but they were mostly young lads who had responded to the call to serve King and country. They had waved goodbye to their wives, sweethearts and friends when they left the Central Station at the Foot of Leith Walk bound for Larbert, to take part in training exercises prior to moving to France, but later, the Battalion was ordered to be included as reinforcement for the Gallipoli campaign. They were scheduled to leave Liverpool on Wednesday 19 May 1915, but the troopship Aquitania had stuck fast in the mud, and departure had been delayed.

Around four o'clock on the morning of 22 May, A and D Companies, comprising the Commanding Officer, Headquarters staff, fifteen officers and 483 other ranks left Larbert by rail for Liverpool. They were in good spirits, and perhaps glad to be on their way at last, and when they stopped for a short spell at Carstairs, wellwishers offered them sweets and cakes to help them on their journey. The troop train had been running late, but on its approach to Carlisle, it began to pick up speed on the down gradient, but at Quintinshill Junction just to the north of Gretna it ploughed into a stationary goods train. Shortly afterwards it was hit by the London to Glasgow overnight express which ran into the wreckage which had been strewn over the tracks, and engulfed the carriages in fire. Doctors and nurses were quickly on the scene, and later an emergency train arrived from Carlisle bringing ambulance staff and more doctors. As the day wore on, local people gathered outside the Drill Hall in Dalmeny Street,

Gretna Disaster : The engine tender of the London Express
after collision with the troop train

16

Leith, anxiously waiting for news, and over one hundred relatives made the journey by special train to Carlisle to visit the injured. 3 Officers, 29 NCO's and 182 men of the Battalion had perished, and 193 were injured. Other casualties involving passengers on the express and railwaymen totalled 15 dead and 55 injured. Those officers and men who had survived the accident spent the night in Carlisle before continuing their journey by train to Liverpool, and they had already embarked before a message was received to say that only the seven officers who had survived were to sail.

Over 120 coffins were brought back to Battalion Headquarters in Dalmeny Street, Leith, and on 25 and 26 May, horse-drawn carriages conveyed them along the route into Leith Walk and via Pilrig Street to Rosebank Cemetery where they were buried with full military honours in mass graves. All Leith fell silent, businesses and shops were closed, traffic was stilled, windows shuttered and blinds drawn, and the community was left in tears.

The trial of those responsible for the accident was held in December 1915, in the High Court of Justiciary in Edinburgh before the Lord Justice General, Lord Strathclyde. The accused were George Meakin, signalman, George Hutchison, fire-man, and James Tinsley, signalman. Meakin was charged with having failed to make use of lever collars as was established practice, and had also failed to give the necessary signals with regard to the shunting procedures of a local passenger train. Hutchison, as fireman of a local passenger train when shunted, was charged with having failed to receive the necessary assurances from the signal box regarding the use of lever collars. Tinsley, who had arrived for duty that morning at 6.30am instead of 6.00am, was charged with having failed to establish the position of the trains, and had accepted the special troop train from Larbert to Carlisle by signalling to the up line signal box that all was clear when in fact, it was not.

Gretna Memorial : Commemorative Plaque at entrance to Rosebank Cemetery

The evidence which was given was much in line with that which had been submitted to the Board of Trade Enquiry, and the defence argued that Tinsley's forgetfulness with regard to the local passenger train was caused by a sudden failure of memory, and was not due to criminal negligence, and therefore should be judged as an unhappy combination of events. The jury took only eight minutes to consider their position, and returned a unanimous verdict of guilty against Meakin and Tinsley, and of not guilty against Hutchison who was discharged. The Defence sought a moderate sentence against the guilty railwaymen, and Lord Strathclyde said that he would not add further to the bitter lifelong remorse that the accused would feel. Meakin was sentenced to eighteen months imprisonment, and Tinsley to three years penal servitude.

A public appeal to the community for £2,000 raised nearly £4,000, and in addition to a memorial, a bed was endowed in Leith Hospital. The memorial itself still stands in Rosebank Cemetery, and is of granite in the style of St Martin's Cross on Iona, and was designed by George Simpson, the Leith Burgh Architect. The Service of Dedication was held on 12 May 1916, when the Earl of Rosebery, Hon. Colonel of the Battalion performed the unveiling before a large crowd. The Battalion's colours now hang in South Leith Parish Church.

Sadly, the story of Leith's 7th Battalion does not end there, as those who had sailed from Liverpool arrived in Gallipoli on 11 June 1915, and by 28 June they were already involved in action. By mid July, the 1028 officers and men who had left Leith with such high hopes had been reduced to 174, and the tall grey tenements and streets from where they came were never to seem the same again.

TWELVE O'CLOCK COACH

Superstition has it that in the old Tolbooth Wynd, the sound of the 'twelve o'clock coach' could be heard, usually around midnight during a storm, or preceding a spell of bad weather. The thundering noise of the coach filled the local inhabitants with fear when the great hearse-like vehicle appeared. Driven by a tall, gaunt figure without a head, and drawn by headless black horses it was said to have been occupied by a mysterious lady.

TRIBUTE TO TANCY

Although it is many years since James 'Tancy' Lee died, he is still recognised as being the first boxer to put Scotland on the fight map. Although remembered as a Leither, Tancy was in fact born in Glasgow in 1882, and served with the King's Own Scottish Borderers during the South African War where he contracted dysentery which reduced his weight to around four stones. He had a talent for boxing, but he was twenty-eight before he won a Scottish Amateur Championship, and a disputed British title in London. He turned professional in 1911, and in 1915, at the age of thirty-three, he beat Jimmy Wilde, ten years his junior, for the British Flyweight Championship. Wilde complained that he had been ill during training, and was not at his best, but Tancy, who had difficulty making the weight, eventually forced the 'Tylorstown Terror' into submission, the referee stopping the fight in the seventeenth round.

Tancy's weight problems continued, and he lost his title in sixteen rounds to Young Symons, and in a rematch with Jimmy Wilde, he lost in eleven rounds. He moved up to bantam weight and knocked out Tony Noble, and then defeated Charlie Hardcastle in four rounds to take the featherweight title. He then won his first Lonsdale belt at that weight outright by defeating Joe Conn and Danny Morgan. The amazing thing about Tancy Lee was that he didn't turn professional until he was nearly thirty years old. He won his last Lonsdale belt when he was thirty-seven, and didn't retire until he was approaching fifty years of age. Some thought that his career might be over when he was beaten by Mike Honeghan in 1920, but in 1926, he returned to the ring and beat a much younger Johnny Sealey at the Waverley Market.

Tancy's style and courage endeared him to his followers, and when he ducked under the ropes at the Waverley Market for the last time, he was given a standing ovation. His early training days were spent at Charlie Cotter's gym in Leith Street, and for several years he was principal instructor at the Leith Victoria Club, before being appointed instructor to the Irish Free Army for a short spell. He came into the fight game when the Welsh School was dominant, with boxers like Jimmy Wilde and Jim Driscoll, but although Scottish boxing was not in the top rank, Tancy's success inspired others, and sports followers began to sit up and take notice. His nephew George Mackenzie, together with Alex Ireland, came to the fore in the formation of the Leith School, and with the Hamilton School in the West, began to wrest the dominance in boxing from Wales and France.

James 'Tancy' Lee lived most of his life in Easter Road in Leith, but at 9.25pm on February 5 1941, when returning from fire fighting duties, he was fatally injured by a bus in Duncan Place. So passed a true gentleman whose skills and courage in the ring have never been truly recognised.

ACROSS THE RIVER

The first bridge across the Water of Leith is recorded as having been built by Robert Ballantyne, an Abbot of Holyrood in 1493. This was located some 100 yards up-river from the present Sandport Bridge, and is no longer in existence.

Two new types of bridge were built around the 1800s. The first, the Sandport Bridge at Tolbooth Wynd, had two side spans built of stone, with an opening

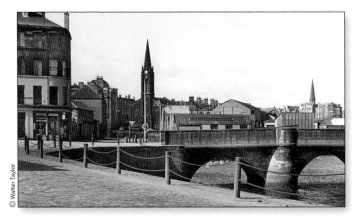

© Walter Taylor

The Coalhill : The Sandport Bridge at the corner of Henderson Street and the Coalhill with the former St Thomas' Church in the background

section of two half spans, hinged at the ends, and lifted by winches and ropes. This bridge was built around 1788, and it seems likely that the centre spans were originally of timber.

A second bridge, on the line of Bernard Street, was built around 1800, and was similar in construction to the Sandport Bridge, but with cast iron lifting sections. This bridge was replaced by a swing bridge, built in 1898, which was strengthened in 1932, and ultimately replaced by a reinforced concrete bridge in 1961, although the original piers still remain.

The Victoria Swing Bridge was a much more sophisticated structure, and was built to a design by AM Rendell of London. It spans a clear channel of one hundred and twenty feet, and was opened in 1874. Built at a cost of around £30,000, it was for a time the largest swing bridge in the country.

ATTEN-SHUN !

If you happen to pass the statue of Queen Victoria at the Foot of Leith Walk, you may stop to read the commemorative panels placed around the stone pedestal. One of these refers to the visit of Queen Victoria to Leith in 1842, but you may have wondered about the reference to the 5th Battalion The Royal Scots.

The story goes back to August 1859, when 153 gentlemen of Leith offered to form two rifle companies, and pay all their own expenses for the privilege of doing so. Shortly afterwards, two companies of Leith artisans were formed, and they paid thirty shillings as a contribution to their expenses, the remainder being defrayed by means of public subscription. In December 1859, the officers were gazetted to the 1st Midlothian (Leith) Rifle Volunteer Corps, comprised of four companies and a brass band. More companies were formed at regular intervals, and by 1861, eight had been formed, all recruited from the Leith area.

By 1884, the Battalion had increased its strength to ten companies, and in 1890, adopted the insignia of the Royal Scots, the helmet continuing to be worn until 1905, when Kilmarnock bonnets were worn by officers, and Glengarries by the

The 7th Battalion Royal Scots on the march through West Linton in 1910

men. The Battalion tartan was the Hunting Stewart.

During the South African War, the Battalion provided 196 men for service, while a further 94 enlisted in the regular army. Captain Campbell and Corporal T. Greig of the 1st Company were mentioned in despatches, and Corporal Greig was also awarded a medal for distinguished conduct in the field. Private J. Lockhart of the 3rd Company was also mentioned in despatches, and promoted to Corporal for gallantry.

The Battalion was further increased to eleven companies in 1900, but in 1901, it was reorganised into ten, one of which was a cycling Company, and it became part of the 32nd Field Army Brigade between the years 1902 and 1906.

In 1877, a headquarters and drill hall were built in Stead's Place at a cost of £3,000, but these were destroyed by fire in 1902, and new premises were built in Dalmeny Street.

During the Royal Review of 1905 in Holyrood Park, the Battalion provided 20 officers and 1,000 men out of a total of 38,383 officers and men on parade on that day. In March 1907, the 5th Volunteer Battalion had an establishment of 1,164 officers and men, but after 1st April 1908, it was converted into the 7th Battalion The Royal Scots, which was to become victim of the horrific rail accident near Gretna in May 1915.

BODY SNATCHERS

References to body snatchers are contained within the registers of South Leith Church, and the height of this ghoulish trade appears to have been during the middle of the eighteenth century. These body snatchers were more commonly referred to as resurrectionists, and they robbed the graves of recent interments and sold them to doctors for medical research.

South Leith and North Leith Churchyards were troubled by these snatchers, and many stories must have been told about the men and vehicles conveying the bodies over the cobbled streets of Leith. Various methods were tried to prevent this practice occurring, and some families inserted metal grilles within the vault openings to keep the snatchers at bay. Watchtowers were also used, but it appears that the watchmen, when on duty, drank a little too much, and were usually in no fit state to defend the graves.

St. Ninian's Churchyard

21

LEITH CENTRAL STATION

The busiest rail terminus in Leith during the heyday of rail networks was Leith Central Station at the Foot of Leith Walk, which has sometimes been claimed as the biggest station built from scratch during the twentieth century. It was opened in 1903 by the North British Company, and occupied a site bounded by Easter Road, Duke Street and Leith Walk.

The unassuming main entrance was located below the present clock tower, but there was also a subway entrance from Easter Road, and a carriageway leading from Leith Walk gave access for vehicles to the heart of the station. The interior was vast by most standards, and comprised four main platforms, each some 790 feet long, and the steel framed, glazed roof varied in width to a maximum of around 220 feet. The signal box at the Easter Road end became a local feature as was the rather delicate glazed elevation facing East. Fronting Duke Street and Leith Walk were shops, pubs and restaurants at ground level, and at first floor level the waiting rooms and general offices served the station. The clock tower over the front entrance has become something of a local landmark, thanks to the Town Council of the time which insisted that one should be placed there.

Leith Central Station : The fine glazed elevation viewed from Easter Road

There is no clear reason why North British committed such a large station to Leith, but perhaps it had something to do with stifling the Caledonian Railway's ambitious development plans for the area at that time. During the early years, however, the station exceeded expectations, and the seven-minute journey to Waverley via Abbeyhill became very popular. The journey to Musselburgh took twenty-one minutes, including stops, and some through trains to Glasgow also left Leith Central. One of the situations which probably influenced users of the service during the early years was the problem with tram cars at Pilrig, the notorious 'Pilrig Muddle', where passengers had to change from electric to cable-operated cars during the journey to and from Edinburgh. However, after the amalgamation with Edinburgh in 1920, the tram car service was unified, rail passenger numbers dropped significantly, and Leith Central closed to passenger traffic in 1952, less than fifty years after opening. It was used until 1972 as a diesel maintenance depot and driving school, and lay derelict for many years under the ownership of the District Council. The station was demolished in 1989.

© Walter Taylor

The Carriageway : The goods entrance to the station from Leith Walk to the main platforms

During its relatively short life, the platforms of Leith Central Station serviced many of the locomotives and express trains of the day, but now, where the sounds and smells of steam and diesel would once be encountered, the comparative quiet of a Scotmid supermarket and Waterworld complex house only the ghosts of these earlier years.

CROMWELL'S ARCH

Squeezed alongside the old Mariners' Church at the bottom of Dock Street lies what was once the main entrance port to the famous fortress of Leith. It consists of an elliptical arch, nine feet high and thirty feet deep, and once had a tenement on top, which is believed to have been a later addition. It traces back in time to the Commonwealth, when Edinburgh and Leith were occupied by Cromwell's troops after the defeat at the Battle of Dunbar, and formed one of five fortresses ordered to be built in Scotland to be garrisoned by Cromwell's troops.

This was a task which was left to General Monk, and it was under his supervision that the Citadel in North Leith was built. It was located near to the western edge of the old fortifications which had been built during the Siege of Leith, on

© Walter Taylor

Cromwell's Arch : The East gate of the fortification looking through to Dock Street

the site of St. Nicholas' Church, which had to be demolished. At that time it commanded the entrance to the harbour, in a key position to resist any attack which might have been made on Edinburgh.

The fortress itself was pentagonal in shape, and consisted of three bastions and two platforms, with the wall running along the approximate line of Coburg Street until it took a westerly line parallel to Couper Street, where it continued for a short length until it turned down to the sea. Within the fortress were the barracks, officer's quarters, the General's house, a chapel, armoury and magazine. The walls were constructed of stone, hewn on both faces and surrounding the walls was a ditch. The Magistrates of Edinburgh were somewhat unhappy with the building of the fortress, fearing that their superiority over Leith would be undermined, but matters were eventually settled when General Monk received £5,000 towards the cost of the fortress, which is recorded as having taken £100,000 to build.

After the completion of the Citadel, there followed a period of some prosperity, but this was not to last, and orders were given for it to be demolished. The Duke of Lauderdale managed to purchase the buildings from the Magistrates of Edinburgh, and the fortifications were only partially demolished, and some houses were left intact. Several Lords and Ladies had houses within the Citadel, but by 1800, aristocratic residents had given way to the keepers of summer bathing quarters, to be used by the citizens making use of the fine beach at the Short Sands. Macintosh of Borlam made his quarters in the Citadel during the Jacobite rising of 1715, and he improved the defences against the Duke of Argyll, who marched on the Citadel with 1,000 men and demanded surrender, which was rejected.

Macintosh fled over the sands to Seton, and the Citadel was left in much the same condition as he had left it, until towards the end of the eighteenth century when Rennic's plans for the new docks were introduced.

The Statistical Account for Scotland 1793, describes three of the bastions, and two of the gates that were still standing, but these were later removed, and now, all that remains is the one gate which bridges the gap between Leith's historic past and the new Leith.

KULTUR PANEL

There is a building in Pitt Street, Leith, which many people may pass by and be somewhat puzzled by a moulded feature at high level bearing the inscription 'The Valour of German Culture.' When this building was built in 1915, it was thought that the feature would provide a source of curiosity for future generations, and many have wondered as to its origin.

Kultur Panel : A Memorial to Belgian civilians who suffered at the hands of Germans during the First World War

It was referred to as a 'German Kultur' panel, and was the work of Mr William Baxter who produced copies of the panel in England and Wales around the same time.

It contains no fewer than eighteen figures, formed in terra cotta from a clay model, and is meant to portray the cruelty of German soldiers towards the Belgian people during the First World War. The plight of the helpless mothers and their children can be easily identified, as can the sight of a German soldier bearing his Iron Cross.

The panel was intended to raise antagonism against the Germans during the war, and assist in the recruitment of men into the forces.

TRAINING SHIP DOLPHIN

HMS Dolphin was built in Middlesborough by Dixon & Company in 1882. Technically, she was a ship of composite construction, with a four inch thick mahogany hull, sheathed with a further two inches of teak, and lined below the water line with heavy gauge copper plating. In addition to a full suit of sails, she was propelled by a steam engine, and was commissioned at Sheerness in 1884 as an auxiliary barque of 925 tons displacement.

TS Dolphin : Berthed beside the Custom Quay before being taken to the breaker's yard at Bo'ness

She was first assigned to the Mediterranean Squadron, and took part in the defence of the Red Sea port of Suakin near Port Sudan, where the army was being besieged by local tribesmen. In1885 the tribesmen were driven off by *Dolphin's* guns, which were assisted by a new feature in warfare, namely the searchlight, which was used for the first time on record. In 1896, *Dolphin* was laid up at Sheerness, and had her guns stripped and taken ashore. Her engine was also removed, and she became part of the Sail Training Squadron at Portland. Some ten years later, *Dolphin* was taken to Gosport to become the first Submarine Depot Ship, and eventually became the flagship of the Officer Commanding Submarines at Fort Blockhouse. In 1942, *Dolphin* was offered for sale, and was purchased by Sir Donald Pollock, the Chairman of Metal Industries, with the intention of using it as a boys' club in Leith. Unfortunately, on tow to Leith in bad weather she became awash, and threatened to sink, but the tug Captain managed to beach her at Fisherrow. She was salvaged some months later, put into dry dock and refitted by Sir Donald at his yard at Rosyth. The refitted *Dolphin* returned to Leith in 1928, and was berthed in the West Old Dock, and served mainly as a boys' club, but was also used for training boys who wished to go to sea.

The Second World War restricted access to the docks and to the ship, but in 1944, when Leith Nautical College was searching for additional accommodation,

Dolphin was used to introduce a deck boys' course. This was followed some two years later by a catering course, and the main deck midships was converted into an instruction galley where ships' cooks were trained by staff of Edinburgh College of Domestic Science.

In 1965, when the West Old Dock was infilled, *Dolphin* was towed to the East Old Dock, and later she was given her last berth near to Bernard Street bridge where it was hoped she could give several more years service to seafarers. This was not to be, however, and in 1977, when the new College was opened in Milton Road, Edinburgh, *Dolphin* made her last voyage to the breaker's yard at Bo'ness.

PICTURE HOUSES

The first moving pictures in Edinburgh are said to have been shown at a fairground in Iona Street in 1893, but Leith's first picture house was probably Falconers, which operated from a tent in Jane Street around 1899, and is said to have shown short films of notable events of the day. Many may remember the Laurie which was located on the area now occupied by the yard behind Woolworth's at the Foot of Leith Walk. This opened in 1911, and during its lifetime was known by several names such as Leith Picture House, the Laurie Picture House, and the Alison. It was also known as the 'flea box', and rumour said that you could gain entry in exchange for a jam jar. The Laurie closed after the Second World War with a showing of *Power Dive* featuring Richard Arlen.

Also opened in 1911 was the Imperial Picture House in Storrie's Alley off the Kirkgate, where an extrovert Manager called Captain Texas was said to have shot cards and clay pipes from his daughter's mouth during the interval. Around 1912, there was a cinema in Parliament Street which operated under the name of The Magnet, and this consisted of an iron shed with a seating capacity of some 200. Further along the street at Coalhill/Henderson Street stood the Cinema House which opened in April 1913. This cinema was well appointed, and could seat up to 600 persons. It stood empty for part of the first world war years, but reopened in 1917 as the Empire Picture House. This cinema closed around 1930, but the moulded stone supports for the roof structure can still be seen at Coalhill.

On New Years Day 1913, the Palace at the Foot of Leith Walk opened, which at the time rivalled some of the best cinemas in Edinburgh. The design of this cinema was quite unusual, and the building can still be identified as a former picture house. The Palace closed in December 1966 with the final show featuring Rosalind Russell and Hayley Mills in *The Trouble with Angels*.

The Alhambra Picture House in Leith Walk had a classical frontage, and much ornate plaster work internally. It was designed by Leith Architect James Johnston, and was originally opened as a Palace of Varieties in December 1914, but was mainly used as a cinema. The Alhambra closed in March 1958, and the building was demolished in 1974.

Picture Houses : The Alhambra Cinema in Leith Walk,
closed in 1958, and was demolished in 1974

The Capitol in Manderston Street was one of the biggest cinemas of the time with a seating capacity of 2,300. It closed as a cinema in July 1961, but had a new organ installed for its bingo goers in 1979.

The last picture house to be built in Leith was the State in Great Junction Street which opened in December 1938. This was a luxury super cinema, seating around 1500, and was built as part of a complex comprising shops, two billiard saloons and a skittles alley. The sound system was the most up to date available, and the building remains as a good example of the last of the picture houses. The last show was presented in May 1972, when Clint Eastwood and Richard Burton appeared in *Where Eagles Dare.*

The Gaiety was originally built as a theatre, and dated from 1888 when it was known as the Princess's Theatre. It was named the Gaiety in 1913 when it was extended, and was used as a cinema for some thirty years before variety returned towards the end of the Second World War. The last theatre production was with Johnny Beattie and the Four Kordites, and the building was demolished in the 1960's as part of the redevelopment of Leith.

EARLY RAILWAY DAYS

Around 150 years ago, the first of our local railway systems were stretching into Leith and Granton, and we now have the benefit of strolling along the routes of some of these lines which have been made into pleasant walkways. The earliest of these lines was obtained by Act of Parliament in 1836 on behalf of the Edinburgh, Leith and Newhaven Railway, but difficulties with the construction of the tunnel running through the New Town ran the Company into financial problems. The scheme was abandoned, but a route from Scotland Street to Trinity was opened in 1842. An extension to the pier at Granton was opened in 1846, and later that year the line to the Citadel or North Leith Station was completed.

The tunnel section between Scotland Street Station and Canal Street posed a huge problem, but was eventually completed in 1847, and was an extraordinary engineering achievement for the time. The tunnel measured 1,052 yards with a steep incline, and passed below Scotland Street, Drummond Place, Dublin Street and St Andrew Square before emerging at Canal Street, with the mouth set below the level of Princes Street. The incline unfortunately was too steep for the locomotives of the day, and carriages had to be drawn by cables from Scotland Street Station by means of a winding machine at Canal Street. This machine was built by Hawthorn of Leith, and youngsters used to watch the wire cable being hooked to the carriages at Scotland Street, and when a signal was passed to Princes Street that the carriages were ready, a warning bell would sound, and they would disappear into the gloom of the tunnel.

On the down slope, the descent was made by means of brake wagons, and passengers and brakemen had to endure the showers of sparks and ear-piercing screeches as the carriages made their way to the relative comfort of Scotland Street Station. The wagons for Leith and Granton were firstly drawn by horses to the mouth of the tunnel, and then descended down the incline to the station at Scotland Street where a waiting locomotive was connected, and the train then proceeded through Heriot Hill tunnel, across the Water of Leith, and branched off to the left towards Granton, the main route following the line of the river towards the Citadel station. There was a station between Princes Street and the Citadel, at Bonnington where the station master's house can still be seen below the bridge, and the former station on the bend of the Trinity line also remains.

It was usually a source of some amusement on the Citadel line when the locomotive was disconnected around South Fort Street, and ran on ahead to be shunted for the returning journey. The carriages proceeded on their own, down the incline to the station, with the guard perched on the roof manipulating the brake, and the youngsters thought it great fun to race the train from one side of the road to the other as it passed under Junction Bridge.

These trains were usually of three carriages, comprising first, second and third class, and had no brake van. Luggage was placed on the carriage roof where the guard was also seated, and the service at that time was every hour, with fares of 4 pence, 3 pence and 2 pence for the various classes. Passengers for Granton had to change at Scotland Street, and when it was busy with visitors there was a hustle and bustle when the pier was approached. Shouts of 'the Stirling and Alloa boat this way' could be heard above the din, and this run was served by the steamers Victoria and Prince of Wales. The passage to Stirling was usually uneventful, but occasionally one of the steamers would get stuck in the mud between there and Alloa.

Despite the difficulties faced with the construction of the tunnel to Scotland Street, it was certainly not the answer, and soon the lines to Leith and Granton were re-routed, and a new route to Trinity from Piershill bypassed most of the former Edinburgh, Leith and Granton lines.

FLOATING JOHNNY

The Edinburgh and Leith Seamen's Friend Society was formed in 1820, and its objects were the spiritual and temporal care of seafarers and their dependents. At that time the Society's church was a converted sloop which was moored in the docks, and it came as no surprise to learn that the minister was known locally as 'Floating Johnny.' When this floating chapel became unfit for use, the directors applied to the Admiralty for another sloop, but the cost of conversion proved to be an obstacle. The Directors decided to make a public appeal for funds, with the result that a Mariners' Church was built in Dock Street in 1839.

Floating Johnny : The engraved panel above the entrance to the Mariners' Church in Dock Street

ARTILLERY MOUNDS

The two prominent mounds on Leith Links are known as the Giant's Brae and Lady Fyfe's Brae, and historically they are accepted as artillery mounds, used by the English army during the Siege of Leith in 1560, and now scheduled as Ancient Monuments. But are they?

The original map of the Siege of Leith is held in Petworth House, Sussex, and this map must be regarded as the most definitive record of the time in existence. Referred to as the Petworth Map, the three gunsites known as Mounts Pelham, Somerset and Falcon are clearly shown, but due to foreshortening, and possible inaccuracies in the drawing, the exact locations are unlikely ever to be determined. In 1990, an excellent treatise on the subject was written by the late Stuart Harris, a former City Architect, who raised doubts as to the relevance of these mounds to the Siege of Leith, and supported his argument with measurements and tracings.

The two gunsites on the Links known as Mount Pelham and Mount Somerset were named after Captains in the English army, but these sites in their original form would probably have been temporary forts of some 3 acres in area, with guns capable of firing at ranges up to 500 yards. It was suggested that the more likely locations of these two forts would have been bounding Burns Street and East Restalrig Terrace for Mount Pelham, and around Pilrig Park for Mount Somerset. It seems questionable that the visible mounds on Leith Links have anything to do with the Siege of Leith, and this view was also shared by the late Professor Gordon Donaldson when he presented a report on the Petworth Map to the Old Edinburgh Club in 1966.

LAST PROVOST

Leith's last Provost was John A. Lindsay, CBE., DL., who was born in Leith in 1865. He played a leading part in public life in the Port over many years, and was Provost at the time of the amalgamation with Edinburgh in 1920. He was a founder member of the firm of John and James Lindsay, flour importers, and was a man with many interests. He entered Leith Town Council in 1904, was appointed Treasurer in 1906, and became a Magistrate in 1907. He later became Convener of the Public Health Committee and was elected Provost in 1917.

After the amalgamation with Edinburgh, he was presented with his portrait in oils which still hangs in the Old Council Chamber. For twenty-five years he was on the Board of Management of Leith Hospital, and was President for twelve years. It was largely as a result of his efforts that a sum of £80,000 was raised for the building of the children's wing of Leith Hospital which also stands as the memorial to the Leith men who fell during the First World War. He was elected Chairman of the former Leith Dock Commission in 1935, and was awarded the CBE in 1937 when he was 76 years old. In referring to the death of John Lindsay on 21 April 1942, Lord Provost Will Y Darling recognised the long, faithful service rendered to the Port by the last Provost of Leith.

SHIPS AT WAR

During the First World War, only two small ships were built in Leith shipyards for the Royal Navy, but before the outbreak of the Second World War, the facilities at the Leith yards had been substantially improved, and from the Victoria Shipyards, Henry Robb & Co. built 42 ships for the Royal Navy, 14 merchant ships, and repaired nearly 3,000 ships for the Royal and Merchant Navies during the period from December 1939 until August 1945. These ships included Flower and Castle Class corvettes; River, Loch and Bay Class frigates; Bangor Class minesweepers, and Bustler Class Rescue tugs. The first to be launched were the two trawlers, *HMS Hickory* and *Hazel*, and the last was the frigate *HMS Padstow Bay* which was launched in August 1945.

Orders from the Government of New Zealand included three minesweeper training ships called the *Moa*, *Kiwi* and *Tui*, which were launched during the spring and summer of 1941. These minesweepers operated as part of the 25th Minesweeper Flotilla of the Royal New Zealand Navy, and served in the Solomons and New Caledonia as part of the American Fleet. An incident in 1943 involved the *Kiwi* and *Moa* which had picked up signals from a Class 1 Japanese submarine which was carrying stores and personnel to Guadalcanal. The *Moa* stood off while *Kiwi* carried out a depth charge attack which forced the submarine to surface. The crew from *Kiwi* sprayed the submarine with machine gun fire, and ignoring the return fire from the Japanese gunners, she rammed the submarine three times in rapid succession with *Kiwi* receiving no more than a dented bow. Some months later, the *Moa* was sunk by a direct hit during an air attack whilst at anchor. The *Kiwi* and *Tui* continued their work together, covering a wide area of the Pacific, and only a few weeks after the loss of the *Moa*, another Japanese submarine was depth charged and forced to the surface where it was sunk by American aircraft.

The corvette *HMS Lotus* was responsible for the sinking of the first U-boat in the Mediterranean in April 1943, and shared with the *Starwart* a second victim on the very next day. She also saw service at the siege of Tobruk, and was involved in escort duties to Murmansk on the Russian supply lines.

To the frigate *HMS Nith* fell the distinction of being selected as an HQ ship during the D-Day operations, but she was hit during a bombing attack, and several of the crew were killed. The frigate *HMS Derg* was one of the ships present during the signing of the Japanese surrender in Tokyo Bay, and *HMS Bustler* was one of the tugs responsible for towing the pipelaying drums loaded with steel pipes across the Channel in preparation for the 'Pluto' operation and invasion of Normandy.

One of the more unusual repairs carried out during the war involved *HMS Cossack*. She had been rammed in the dark by a merchant ship in the North Sea whilst on escort duty, and all that had saved her from being cut in two was her gun turret. When she arrived at Leith, she was down some six feet by the head, and the mess decks were awash. Extensive repairs were carried out over a period of five to six weeks, and the ship returned to duty. Soon afterwards however, she returned again to Leith for repairs, but this time under the command of Captain Vian who had lost his own ship the *Elfrida*. The repairs were carried out as a matter of some urgency, and *HMS Cossack* returned to operational duties. She became involved in the boarding of the German supply ship *Altmark* in a Norwegian fjord, and the release of British prisoners of war who were brought back into Leith. As a result of this action, *HMS Cossack* suffered further damage to the bow and side, and for a third time she was repaired in Leith.

THE OPTIMISTS

Leithers have never been noted for their optimistic outlook, but surely the Burghs Pilot summary of the year 1899 was just a little too depressing ?

'This has been a disastrous year for the Port. The whisky crisis has seriously affected business all round, and at the close of the year, Leith, in conjunction with other commercial centres is severely feeling the effects of the War. In every department of trade and commerce, without exception, business has been at a very low ebb. Indeed, not for many years has the Port experienced such a trying time. As regards the public affairs of the Burgh, nothing of outstanding importance falls to be recorded, and in each department of public life, things have been pretty humdrum'.

LEITH LINKS

Leith Links once covered a much larger area of ground than it does today and extended to Restalrig, Lochend, the Figgate Whins, and was open to the sea on its northern fringe. It provided grazing ground for cattle and other animals, and the whins when dried, provided a good supply of fuel for houses and baker's ovens in the town.

It was not until 1856 that the Links came into the possession of Leith, the original superiority belonging to the Logans of Restalrig. In 1555, Mary of Guise purchased the superiority of Leith and the Links from the Logan family for the sum of £3,000 Scots, the money being borrowed from Leithers on the

Home of Golf : The cairn on Leith Links recognising that in 1744 the first official rules of golf were drawn up for a tournament played on Leith Links

understanding that Leith would be made a burgh of barony, and later a royal burgh. This promise was never made good, however, and the money was never repaid. Worse was to follow, as Mary, Queen of Scots inherited the superiority from Mary of Guise on her death, and she mortgaged the superiority to the Magistrates of Edinburgh for 10,000 merks at a time when her own finances were being sorely stretched. Two years later, as the mortgage had not been redeemed, Edinburgh assumed the overlording of Leith and the Links.

This position remained unchanged for almost three hundred years until in 1833, by Act of Parliament, Leith was created a Municipal Burgh with its own Provost, Magistrates and Council. The Links was purchased from Edinburgh Town Council for £625, on the understanding that it would remain 'as an open space in all time coming for the use of the public.' It was on the Links that the young King James IV encamped his troops while awaiting the tragic news of his father after the Battle of Sauchieburn. It was here too that James VI mustered his troops to assist Elizabeth when the country was being threatened by Spain in 1588.

When Charles II came to Scotland and took the National Covenant, Oliver Cromwell marched north, and 40,000 men were mustered on the Links, and formed a defensive wall which Cromwell and his Ironsides could not breach. He tried again, however, when the Scots were defeated at Dunbar, and he reached Edinburgh, and occupied Leith. He housed his artillery in South Leith Church, and for seven years the congregation had to hold their services at Restalrig, or worshipped on the Links using the Giant's Brae as a pulpit. The last occasion that an army was assembled on the Links was in 1745, when Prince Charlie prepared to review his troops prior to marching into England. The guns from Edinburgh Castle, however, forced him to move to Musselburgh where he was out of their reach.

Around 1770, the first houses were erected in the vicinity of the Links, owned mainly by merchants, and in 1806, the Grammar School, or High School of Leith was built on the site now occupied by Leith Primary School. The former church, with its classical frontage, which adjoins the school was built in 1837. In the most southern corner of the Links, where the golf clubhouse once stood, was located Watt's Hospital, named after James Watt, a Leith merchant, who bequeathed it for destitute men and women over fifty years old, who had the surname Watt, were natives of the parish of South Leith, and who were not in receipt of an allowance from any charitable institution except the Parochial Board of South Leith. From 1880, a network of new streets began to spread outwards from the Links, and the long rope walk buildings appeared on the northern edge.

For 350 years, the Links of Leith was one of the best known golf courses in Scotland, and it was here that the first international foursome was played. The first national golf tournament played by professional players was also played over the Links on May 18, 1867. The course at that time comprised of seven holes, and four rounds were played, making twenty-eight holes in total. Large crowds of spectators gathered at the Giant's Brae near to the first tee, and the best round of seven holes was one of twenty-eight strokes. The Links was the original home of the Honourable Company of Edinburgh Golfers who met in taverns in the Kirkgate before the clubhouse was built on the site of the former Watt's Hospital. In some financial difficulty, the Company disposed of the clubhouse, moved to Musselburgh, and then to its present home at Muirfield in 1891. The best known Leith golf club was the Thistle Club which was instituted in 1815, fell into abeyance in 1830, reformed in 1865, and finally dissolved in 1890 when all effects were sold at auction in the clubhouse in John's Place.

By 1904, golf on the Links had become a danger to the public, and it was declared illegal, a new course being provided at Craigentinny in 1907. All that remains to remind us of Leith's importance in the history of golf is the cairn which was erected by the Rotary Club of Leith, and which stands at the junction of Wellington Place and Duncan Place.

PILRIG HOUSE

Near to the old boundary of Edinburgh and Leith stands Pilrig House, once in the possession of the Moneypenny family, the lairds of Pilrig, one of whom was killed during the battle of Pinkie in 1547. In 1623, the lands passed into the hands of Gilbert Kirkwood, a goldsmith, who built the House in 1638. It was of typical Scottish construction, and over one of the window lintels was inscribed G K M F in recognition of the marriage of George Kirkwood to Margaret Foulis of Ravelston. Tradition has it that in one of the small rooms used as a strong room, a fine iron chest was kept, reported to be one of the 'treasure chests' taken from a ship which had sailed with the Spanish Armada.

Pilrig House : Lewis Balfour, the grandfather of Robert Louis Stevenson was born in this house in 1777

The Kirkwood name later disappeared from Pilrig, and in 1717 the lands passed from Sir William Douglas to William Alves, were later sold to Lord Rosebery and then to James Balfour in 1718.

Lewis Balfour, the grandfather of R L Stevenson was born in the House in 1777 and the connection with the Balfour family was to last until 1941.

The House saw frequent changes of use over many years, and vandalism and lack of maintenance brought it to a point where it could not be saved. In 1971, and again a year later, fire destroyed the remaining architectural features, and the walls required to be shored up for safety. The property lay derelict for some time, despite local protests, but in 1985, supported by grants from Edinburgh District Council and Historic Buildings, what remained of the property, and the surrounding land, were developed to form 40 retirement homes and 28 flats.

At the opening ceremony, a plaque was unveiled quoting the following lines from Robert Louis Stevenson's Catriona:

'I came in view of Pilrig, a pleasant, gabled house,
set by the waterside among young brave woods'

THINGS NEVER CHANGE

From the Leith Burghs Pilot 1900:

'The regulation of street traffic in Leith is a duty in which the local authorities do not appear to greatly concern themselves. The streets are left pretty much at the disposal of furious charioteers of the butcher boy and milk vanman class with aspirations to the 'pig skin', who take great delight in furiously pacing their Hawkhill trotters through our thoroughfares, regardless of the rights or safety of our citizens. In the pride of their horsemanship, they career all over the place, urging their steeds to fearsome feats of pacing and trotting, and scattering right and left all who cross their path. Only when someone has been run down and injured do the authorities move and institute a prosecution for furious driving. How many more townsfolk we wonder will require to be maimed before the police make an effort to put a spoke in the wheels of these bounding jockeys?'

THE POORHOUSE

Around the turn of the century, Leith had two Poorhouses. One was located on the site of the former David Kilpatrick School in North Junction Street, which was acquired in 1850 only a few months before Leith Hospital was built on the site at Taylor Gardens. A report made to the Leith Parish Council in 1900 indicated that both Poorhouses were overcrowded, and although temporary arrangements had been made to accommodate the 415 inmates, the situation had become critical, and new premises were urgently required.

Leith Poorhouse : The laying of the commemorative stone by Mr William Taylor JP., Chairman of Leith Parish Council in June 1906

Preliminary investigations were carried out, and it was decided that South Leith Poorhouse should be relocated in a new purpose-built building as soon as possible. Three possible sites were considered, one located at Hawkhill, one at Restalrig House, and on land lying to the east of Restalrig which belonged to the Earl of Moray. After further investigation, the Council decided that negotiations should be made with the owner of the ground at Seafield who was Mr Christie Miller of Craigentinny, whose legal agent was Mr Kekewich of London.

It was eventually agreed that Leith Parish Council would feu twelve and a half acres of ground at Seafield, with a right to purchase within ten years of the date of entry. The Council set up a Building Committee of ten Councillors who were to take responsibility for the new building which was to become the Seafield Poorhouse and Hospital for the Sick Poor, now known as the Eastern General Hospital. Finance was an obstacle however, as under the Poor Law Act of 1845, it was only possible to borrow three times the amount of money raised in the preceding year's assessment, which would have fallen far short of the financing required for the new building.

However, a Private Member's Bill was introduced into Parliament by Mr Munro-Henderson, MP for Leith, seeking powers to borrow up to seven times the amount raised for the relief of the poor during the previous year. Plans for the new building were open to competition, and the best of those submitted were exhibited in premises adjoining the Council's offices, but the winner was not offered the commission due to the proposed costs exceeding the budget figures. A local Leith Architect, Mr JM Johnston was offered the commission, and he prepared the necessary plans which comprised a collection of multi-purpose buildings which are substantially as can be seen today. The new Seafield Poorhouse and Hospital was intended to house 600 persons including children and the sick, but the hospital accommodation was increased by 200 patients at planning stage.

The Council had borrowed £57,000 in order to finance the building which was to be repaid over a period of thirty years at $3\frac{3}{8}$ percent. The foundation stone was laid by Mr William Taylor, JP., Chairman of the Council, on 9 June 1906, and the first inmates were transferred from South Leith Poorhouse in October 1907.

In its later rôle, first as Seafield, and then as the Eastern General Hospital, the buildings have served the local community for many years, and once it housed the only Tropical Diseases Unit in Scotland. Many improvements were made to the Maternity Unit, and a fifty bed unit was opened in 1965. In December 1994, two new operating theatres were opened which took the hospital into a new state-of-the-art age despite the fact that the old theatres, built in the 1940s were still functioning smoothly.

SHELLY COAT

Long before the building of the East Wet Dock, it was believed that a sea demon had made his home on a large rock on the sands near to the Citadel where an evil monster occasionally deposited his coat which was made from sea shells. In order to ward off the evil spirits it was considered to be a daring feat to run round the stone chanting:

> *'Shelly Coat! Shelly Coat! Gang awa' hame.*
> *I cry nae yer mercy, I fear nae yer name.'*

One evening, a local man known as 'English Dick' dared to wager a bet with his friends that he would go alone to the stone and say the verse, and return to the inn to have his bet paid. 'English Dick' however, did not reappear that evening, and in the early morning his friends went to the stone to find him lying unconscious, with both legs broken and his body badly bruised. 'English Dick' recovered, and was encouraged to tell his tale to his friends.

He told of the sound of sea shells, and of a monster who took him to Inchkeith, and let out a laugh that was echoed by the rocks on the Fife shore. He was then pelted with boulders, and eventually carried back to the 'Shelly Coat Stane' where he lay exhausted, until found by his friends. No further stories about the 'Stane' are known, and it was eventually blasted away to make way for the new dock which was opened in 1806.

RACING ON THE SANDS

It is hard to imagine that horse racing was once a very popular sport in Leith, as the fine sandy beaches on which the races were held have now disappeared beneath the land reclamation, and development of the dock area which took place during the nineteenth century. It is also difficult to say when horse racing began in Leith, but the first written mention of the sport is noted in a booklet called the Mercurius Caledonius dated 1661, after the Restoration of Charles II.

Races were run on the wet sands from a point at the foot of Constitution Street, eastwards towards Seafield. The course itself was lined with posts and ropes, and a marker at the far end acted as the turning point for the riders who turned, and then headed towards the stand and the winning line. Races were usually run on the best of three heats, each heat consisting of two circuits of the course so that the eventual winner could have raced some ten to twelve miles, which was hard going for the horses over the wet sand. There were no Jockey Club rules in those days of course, and in the early days they were made by the Town Council, who seemed to be able to change the rules whenever they felt like it.

Two silver cups were given as prizes in 1665, one of which was the original King's Cup, which was later changed to a Gold Plate around 1720. Many other cups were presented to the winners, but these were overtaken by the popularity of Subscription Races, which were purses. Nobility were always to the fore on race days, and James VII, the Earl of Eglinton and the Duke of Buccleuch were frequent attenders. Once, the Duke of Hamilton won a sum of one hundred guineas, and gave the entire amount to aid the construction of the observatory on Calton Hill.

The Leith Race Week was usually staged at the end of July, and started with a civic procession from Edinburgh down to Leith. Each morning of the week, one of the uniformed town officers proceeded from the Council Chambers to Leith carrying a flag bedecked pole. Behind him came the City Purse, accompanied by a file of the City Guard, complete with fixed bayonets, and followed by a drummer who beat out a marching rhythm. Many people gathered along the streets to view the parade, and as it proceeded down Leith Walk it inevitably gathered bands of marchers behind it in what was locally known as '*gaun doon wi' the Purse.*' Soon, all that could be seen was the bobbing pole of the town officer as it made its way towards the sands. There was great activity on the sands too, as long lines of gaily coloured tents and booths stretched along the shoreline, and the crowds passed in and out of these local drinking places with increasing regularity.

Sideshows were everywhere, and each day seemed to end with drunkenness and disorder. Saturday became the most outrageous day of the week, and despite appeals being made to the Dock Commission to refuse permissions for the sale of drink, these sad scenes continued. William Hutchison in his '*Tales and Traditions of Leith,*' describes the scenes as whole streets of drinking booths and tents on the sands. For a whole week, the town was one continuous scene of racing and drinking, and the sports were usually concluded by a general demolition of the booths and fighting amongst those who, in spite of whisky and previous fist encounters, were still able to keep their legs.

From starting as a healthy outdoor spectator sport, the Leith Races became an excuse for drinking, fighting and vandalism, and it came as a relief to some people in Leith, but not all, when the races were moved to Musselburgh in 1816.

The sands had finally been declared as unsuitable for racing, and the flat course at Musselburgh was a great improvement. However, the new location did not manage to attract the crowds that Leith had, and in 1836 the Races returned to Leith, and continued until 1859, when the last meeting took place.

Robert Fergusson, the poet, seemed to have an affection for the Port and used 'Leith Races' to paint a vivid picture of the celebrations. Perhaps the following verse may express his feelings at what he saw :

> The races ower, they hale the dools
> Wi' drink o' a' kinkind;
> Great feck gae hirplin hame, like fools,
> The cripple lead the blind.

EARLY SHIPBUILDING

At the turn of the nineteenth century, there was an annual expedition of whalers from Leith to the waters around Greenland and the Davis Strait. Conditions must have been extremely severe for the men aboard, but when they arrived back in Leith, they were given a great welcome. The owners of the majority of vessels at that time were Peter and Christopher Wood, who owned the *Royal Bounty* and the *Raith*, and many others, but the most remarkable boat was the *William and Ann*, which was built in 1759, and had a pink painted stern which had been the fashion at the time. She was one of the Leith fleet in 1803, and continued until 1842 when she and her crew were lost.

William Sibbald & Co. traded with the West Indies in sugar and rum, and their vessels included the *Isabella Simpson*, *Lady Forbes* and the *Roselle*. They had an office in the Kirkgate, and 'Sibbald's Bonds' in the docks were well known at that time, but the business appears to have closed in 1826. The American Company was formed in 1822, and many Edinburgh and Leith merchants took up shares in it. Trading was usually with Sydney direct, carrying cargo and passengers from Leith, and returning with produce. The Company operated four large vessels named the *Triton*, *Greenock*, *Portland* and the *City of Edinburgh*. Their office was located on the north side of the Upper Drawbridge. American timber-built ships were also to be seen in the Port around this time, and these included the *Monarch*, *Columbus*, *Bogle* and *Harmony*.

The Leith, Hamburg & Rotterdam Shipping Co. owned several vessels which were mainly fast sailing schooners, and these included the *Edina*, *Elbe*, *Glasgow* and the *Leipsig Packet*. It was Mr John Davidson who was the first owner to introduce the screw propeller on the Hamburg passage, and this was on the *Conside*, which was later replaced by the screw steamers *Border Queen* and *Ivanhoe*. The Leith, Hull & Hamburg Shipping Co. used two paddle steamers named the *Martello* and the *Mercator*, and these were barque-rigged with square sails. The first vessel to set sail from Leith to Calcutta was a small brig of only 140 tons called the *Louisa*, and this was in 1828.

Among the shipbuilders of the time, Robert Menzies & Co. were building many fine ships, including the brig *Sceptre* and the smack *Royal Sovereign*. At that time too, Sime & Ranken were building from a yard opposite the Old Custom House, and in 1826 launched a large West Indiaman named the *Arcturus*, which sailed to Jamaica on her maiden voyage. She was registered as a Ship of some 364 tons, and was 107 feet long. Thomas Morton's yard around this time was located just below Junction Bridge, on the area which we now know as Coalie Park, where the famous patent slip was erected.

Another firm of shipbuilders called Lachlan Rose & Son was also very active at this time, and operated from a yard above the Upper Drawbridge. Anderson's yard was situated on the south bank of the river, above Sheriff Brae, and in 1827 built one of the largest vessels of the time called *Gladstones*, which was sold to London and Liverpool owners. The Old Shipping Company operated with seven smacks, including the *Duke of Buccleuch* and the *Wellington*. These vessels had a broad band of white painted on the sides, and were known as the 'white siders'. The London & Edinburgh Shipping Co. also had seven smacks in 1828, including the *Robert Bruce* and *Superb* and were known as the 'red siders'. The London, Leith, Edinburgh & Glasgow Shipping Co. had nine vessels including the *Edinburgh Castle, Venus, Hawk* and others, and with their green stripe were known as the 'green siders'. During February 1831, one of their vessels called the *Czar* was lost on Seaforth Rocks, to the east of North Berwick, and many of the crew and passengers were lost.

ELECTRIC OR CABLE

There were no regular transport services in Leith during the early part of the nineteenth century when stagecoaches were the principal mode of travel. After the North Bridge was completed and Leith Walk formed, a regular service was run between the High Street and The Shore, and the horse-drawn omnibus began to replace the stagecoach as the mode of travel. The Edinburgh Provisional Order of 1867 allowed for the licensing of public conveyances, and a further Act passed in 1870 gave local authorities permission to construct tramway systems, which could not, however, be operated without the approval of the Board of Trade.

In 1871, the Edinburgh Tramways Act authorised the Edinburgh Street Tramways Company to construct tramway systems, and various routes were designated, including those between Register House and Bernard Street, and also between the Foot of Leith Walk and Charlotte Street. These services proved to be popular, and a branch between the Foot of Leith Walk and Junction Bridge was also opened.

Edinburgh Town Council had hoped to take over all operations within the City, but Leith Councillors wanted further discussion on the matter as they did not consider that a jointly run system was workable, and wanted to know how this would be administered. Leith eventually entered into a separate agreement with the Edinburgh Street Tramways Company for the continuation of their service within the Burgh. This was a difficult time for Leith, as Edinburgh was also attempting to annexe the Burgh, and impose a cable-run system in the area.

Leith opinion favoured electric traction for the future, and were willing to put up with a further period of horse-drawn vehicles until the new system was constructed.

In January 1905, thirty-one open top, and six closed top trams were ordered, and in August 1905, a service of eight trams was run over the route Leith Walk, Pilrig Street, Newhaven Road and Stanley Road. Further sections were passed by the Board of Trade, and opened later in September. The official opening ceremony took place on 3rd November 1905, when five trams, all decorated with flowers and placards, left the depot in Leith Walk for a trip over the main sections of the system. Provost Mackie was there, as well as representatives from Leith Town Council, Edinburgh Town Council, the Chamber of Commerce and other bodies. The Provost addressed a large crowd assembled at the Foot of Leith Walk, and officially opened the system, whereupon they retired to Smith's Rooms in Duke Street to continue the celebrations.

The new system proved to be very successful, and by 1911 the operating expenses were reported as low, and further extensions were considered. After the end of the First World War, however, costs were difficult to contain, fares began to rise, and the amalgamation with the City of Edinburgh eventually took place in November 1920. As a result of this, Leith tramways merged with the Edinburgh system, and the Leith Manager, Mr. F A Fitzpayne was appointed as Deputy Manager on the new board.

MARY OF GUISE

Mary of Guise was the wife of King James V, and Queen Regent of Scotland. After her death in 1561, her body was taken from the chapel of St. Margaret in Edinburgh Castle to Leith, where it was shipped to France and buried in the nunnery of St. Peter of Rheims. Mary had been forced to take refuge in the Castle after the Reformation, and there she had taken ill. Her body was placed in a lead-lined coffin until it was safe to ship it to France, and her death also signalled the end of the French garrison from Leith, and the removal of the fortifications.

MARY, QUEEN OF SCOTS

In 1561, Mary, Queen of Scots landed at Leith after an absence of thirteen years. Her arrival was delayed by fog in the Firth of Forth, but by early morning, the sun had broken through, and all seemed well. Holyroodhouse, unfortunately, was not quite prepared for her arrival, and tradition has it that she is believed to have spent some time in the house of Andrew Lamb on The Shore, where she met with her supporters. Later that evening, the people of Edinburgh entertained Mary with a mixture of ballads and psalm, which were described as being in much bad taste.

LEITH FORT

In September 1779, the *Le Bon Homme Richard*, under the command of Captain John Paul Jones, and two French ships named the *Pallas* and the *Vengeance*, sailed up the Forth heading for Leith, with the intention of collecting £200,000 from the authorities, and if refused, they would destroy the Port of Leith. Fortunately, the town was saved when a storm blew up forcing the ships to change course. The British Government had repeatedly neglected Scotland in home defence, but now felt that it was time to build a Fort at Leith, and man it with regular artillery. That task fell to James Craig who had prepared plans for the New Town, and who now prepared plans for the new Fort in 1780.

The first Royal Artillery Company to occupy the Fort marched from Perth to man the fortifications in 1793. From that time, at the beginning of the Napoleonic Wars, the blue-coated Companies of the Royal Artillery garrisoned the Fort for over one hundred and fifty years.

© Walter Taylor

Leith Fort : The guardhouse at the entrance to the housing development of Leith Fort built 1957/63

When a Regiment arrived in Edinburgh for a period of duty at the Castle, a detachment was sent to Leith Fort to support the Royal Artillery, and in 1810, a detachment of the Edinburgh Militia was stationed at the Fort. At certain periods, a detachment of infantry was also garrisoned there, and on occasion more than one Company of the Royal Artillery. Captain Patterson's Company of the 2nd Battalion Royal Artillery was stationed at Leith Fort from August 1811 until March 1817, and many of these gunners would have been on active service against the French and their allies at some period during the Napoleonic Wars.

Throughout the 1800s, the Fort was garrisoned by units of the Royal Artillery, and carried out many duties in addition to their day-to-day tasks. They placed their fire engines at the disposal of the Leith Fire Brigade, and in 1824 went to

43

the assistance of Edinburgh Fire Brigade when the Great Fire threatened the Old Town. They manned the Martello Tower from time to time, and in 1861, a time service was set up by Colonel McShan, Commanding Officer Royal Artillery at Leith Fort, who gifted a gun to Edinburgh, which was to be fired six days a week at one o'clock from the Half Moon Battery at Edinburgh Castle. A new Barrack Block was built at the Fort in 1903 in addition to the three existing blocks.

After the First World War, No. 21 Company of the Royal Garrison Artillery left the Fort in 1921, and in April 1925, 37 Heavy Battery of Royal Artlillery arrived at the Fort, followed by 35 Heavy Battery one month later. In 1927, Forth Heavy Brigade Royal Artillery (TA) based at Easter Road, took over the defence of the Forth. The TA Regiment was superseded by the newly formed Royal Artillery HQ, and Direct Establishment (Forth) based at Leith Fort. During the two Great Wars, the Fort was occupied by Royal Artillery Field Defences, nerve centre of Scottish Party HQ, and Forth Fire Command. Detachments of the Royal Army Service Corps, and Royal Army Pay Corps were also billeted at the barracks. Before the Second World War, 50 Company Royal Army Service Corps was stationed at the Fort until the 1950s. The Royal Army Pay Corps were the last unit to leave Leith Fort, when 100 officers and men of the Corps gave their last parade at the barracks in April 1956, which marked the end of the occupation of the Fort after 163 years connection with Leith.

THE KING'S WARK

King James I had many interests in Leith and his founding of the Hospital of St. Anthony was not an isolated gesture. He saw many advantages in having a residence in the area which could be used for royal occasions and the storage of goods and arms for which he was paying rent in local premises. Building started in 1434, but King James had been dead for over sixty years before the building was completed. In 1544 it was burned down by the Earl of Hertford as his forces stormed through the Port and all that remained was a tower located on the north-east corner of the site. The King's Wark, or Palace, was partially rebuilt in 1561/4 by John Chisholme, Queen Mary's Comptroller of Artillery, and in 1575 it was used as a hospital for those who were suffering from the effects of the plague.

With the Union of the Crowns, the King's Wark became less important as an asset, and in 1604, Bernard Lindsay was given part of the property by James VI. Lindsay was a valet to King James and he married Barbara Logan and became a man of some substance. Lindsay improved The Shore by building a 'piazza' which featured pillars and areas of polished stone and benches to serve as an exchange for merchants. Bernard's brother Robert also owned an interest in the property, but Bernard ran out of money and was unable to keep the 'great cellar' in good enough repair for the storage of wines and provisions and Lindsay had to mortgage part of the cellar to clear his financial burden.

A dispute arose between Bernard Lindsay and the Town Council over the boundaries of the Wark and the Earl of Dunfermline was called in to act as Arbiter. The problem was resolved as the King and his courtiers were able to play tennis there in 1617. Six years later, the King's Wark was made into a free bailiary with Bernard Lindsay as the hereditary bailie, and this freed him from any further interference from the Town Council.

After Bernard Lindsay's death, his eldest son Captain Thomas Lindsay retained the Wark for some time but he too got into financial difficulties and finally sold out to William Dick who was later to become Sir William Dick of Braid. The Wark was purchased by the Town Council in 1647, and in 1649 the property was repaired and converted into a weighhouse, and Weighhouse Wynd came to be known as Bernard Street after Bernard Lindsay. The original Wark was destroyed by fire in the 1690's but the remaining building was restored by Robert Hurd and Partners in 1971/8.

NEW COURSE

By the turn of the twentieth century it had become clear that the game of golf could no longer be played over the Links of Leith. The game had become no more than a public nuisance, and had so many restrictions placed upon it that there was considerable pressure for the development of a new course. This was not to be in Leith, however, but at Craigentinny, where land was leased by the Town Council in 1907, and a start made on the construction of a new nine-hole course under the experienced eye of Mr. Ben Sayers.

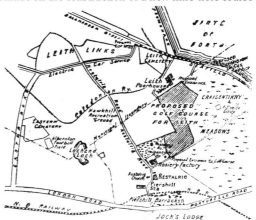

The new clubhouse was situated on the high ground beside the present eighteenth tee, and was reached by steps from the main entrance at Seafield. The clubhouse was timber-built, and provided facilities for both male and female golfers. The first hole was played along the line of the old Leith Poorhouse, the Eastern General Hospital, and played in an anticlockwise direc-

New Golf Course : Plan showing the layout of the new nine-hole course at Craigentinny opened in 1908

tion, skirting Restalrig House, and finishing in front of the clubhouse. The par for the nine holes was reckoned to be around forty-one, but it was expected that there would be many more strokes than that played when the course was opened in 1908.

45

SCOTLAND'S OLDEST STATION

The claim to have possessed the first passenger railway station in Scotland can fairly be made by Leith. This was located in a corner of the dock area at the foot of Constitution Street adjoining the main gates. It served the community until 1903, when Leith Central Station was opened., but continued to serve as a siding facility for the docks. The station master's house was still occupied into the 1950s until it was demolished.

In 1831, the Edinburgh and Dalkeith Railway, having a spur to Fisherrow Harbour, opened its line to Niddrie. The facilities at Fisherrow, however, proved to be insufficient to cope with the increasing demand from the Lothian coalfields, and it was decided to construct a new branch from Niddrie Junction to Leith in order to service the rapidly expanding shipping traffic in the docks.

A local landmark : The diner at the bottom of Constitution Street beside the dock gates

The motive power for the train at that time was the horse, and the rule was one horse to one vehicle which was called the dandy coach. Because of its 'horse power' and freedom from accidents, the line became known as the Innocent Railway. No platform or ticket office was required at the Leith Station as the passengers simply clambered up the footboards and sat on hard wooden seats in the coach, which was open to all types of weather.

In the early 1840s, the North British Railway had established a main line between Edinburgh and Berwick, and then acquired the Edinburgh and Dalkeith line as an asset. Two years later, South Leith terminus was given a new station with all facilities, when steam trains were introduced and the service improved.

The passenger service on the Innocent section of the line was never economic, and was eventually closed. Soon afterwards, the Leith station fell into disuse and was also closed.

TALL SHIPS

One of the finest iron sailing ships ever built in a Leith yard was the 3,102 ton *Drumrock*, which was fitted out by Ramage & Ferguson as a windjammer, and set up some good sailing performances in her early days, managing Dover to Valparaiso in 71 days. In her old age, she sailed under the Canadian flag, and was converted into a barge at Vancouver in 1925. Early in 1927, in course of tow, she ran onto rocks in Queen Charlotte Sound, broke her back, and became a total loss.

Another iron four-masted barque built by Ramage & Ferguson in 1891, was the *Trade Winds*. She was considered to be the finest and biggest ship ever built in Leith at that time, and had a gross tonnage of 2,859 tons. She was intended for the Calcutta jute trade, and her best passage was some 107 days from Hamburg to Calcutta, made in 1892. In 1897, *Trade Winds* sailed under the flag of J Joyce and Company, but ten years later, under German owners, her name was changed to *Magdalene*. Just before the outbreak of the First World War, her name was changed again, this time to *Ophelia*, and during the war she was interned at Caleta Coloso. After the war, she was allocated to the French under the Treaty, but in 1922 was sold back to German owners and broken up at Wilhelmshaven.

Tall Ship : The Crown of India at the quayside

Three-masted barques of 2,000 tons were never popular, because the sail spread was considered to be insufficient for a vessel running to 280 feet long or so. However, three large three-masted barques were built by Ramage & Ferguson to a design by John S Croudace. These were *Castor*, launched in 1886, the *Orion* in 1890 and the *Procyon* in 1892. They were practically sister ships, and sailed under the house flag of WS Croudace of Dundee. The *Procyon* made a speedy maiden voyage under Captain Dundas, and sailed from Leith to New York in fifteen days. The *Orion* was wrecked in January 1906, the *Procyon* was sold to the Russians in 1910, and the oldest, *Castor*, was sold to the Germans in 1911 for breaking up.

An iron four-masted barque of 2,056 tons was built by Ramage & Ferguson in 1885 for the Crown Line, and was named the *Crown of India*. Built for Robertson, Cruickshank & Co., of Liverpool she was sold with three others vessels to J R Young in 1902, and was later owned by J Joyce & Co. She was sunk by a German submarine in 1916.

THE BAKER'S BOY

A story noted from a popular Sunday paper concerned a sixteen year old lad called Anstruther Smith, more popularly known as Ernie, who worked as a baker's boy in Leith. He was too young to join up, but joined the ARP as a Warden and insisted that he was going to bring a medal home to his Mum. During an air raid in 1941, whilst on duty, he comforted a young mother in an underground shelter, and looked after the baby until she had recovered. In April 1941, with the sound of bombers above, Ernie was again escorting local people into the air raid shelter behind Leith Town Hall, when the sound of bombs dropping was heard. He hurried the last person to safety, but a bomb exploded just yards away from him, and the blast threw him down the steps of the shelter. When the dust had cleared, they found Ernie lying dead amongst the debris. A few days later, the baker's boy was buried in Seafield Cemetery, his coffin draped with the Union Jack.

He never managed to bring back that medal which he had promised his Mum, but his selfless regard for his own life on that day has not been forgotten.

COALHILL

In the early part of the nineteenth century, the Coalhill had become one of the most unpleasant localities in Leith. Many of the houses were in a ruinous condition, and the area was the habitual gathering place for wandering outcasts. It was also said to have been the favourite haunt of disembodied spirits, and was without doubt a most unsavoury locality.

*Coalhill : A blacksmith's shop photographed from the quayside
with the tenements of Henderson Street in the background*

Despite the rather squalid background, the Coalhill reveals several interesting historical facts, one of these being the site of the former Council Chamber where the Earls of Lennox, Mar and Morton plotted treason against the Crown. It is said that the building was erected by Mary of Lorraine as the meeting place for her Privy Council. In his 'History of Leith', Campbell writes that in 1827 it still exhibited many traces of regal splendour, and the whole building, both from internal and external appearances was remarkable. Unfortunately, it was demolished as part of an improvement scheme for the area in the mid 1800's, and now provides the site for a modern housing development.

Another important figure of his day who had associations with the Coalhill was Hugh Miller, the celebrated geologist, writer and newspaper editor, who was born in Cromarty in 1802, and whose burial in the Grange Cemetery was witnessed by hundreds of admirers. Hugh Miller was a stonemason, and he came to Leith from Cromarty on the death of his father when at sea. Before setting out on what proved to be his last voyage, his father had fallen heir to a ground floor property in Leith, which was valued at around four hundred pounds. There were debts on the property, however, which Hugh's mother cleared off from the money paid to her under the insurance due from the sinking of his father's vessel. The property had been used for some time as a Spirit Shop and Tavern, and had brought in a good rental, but shortly after the death of his father, an alteration to the harbour dues changed the fortunes of the property which suffered a drastic reduction in the rental being received. The property went into decline, and lost its character, and lay empty for some years. Some said it was then occupied by a ghost which caused problems with the neighbours until it was exorcised by a local police officer.

In May 1824, Hugh Miller sailed into Leith in order to try to sell the property, and also to find work. The property which he had come to sell was by then in a dreadful state of repair, but he made contact with the Town Clerk, Mr Veitch, with whom his father had placed his will shortly before his death. Through Mr Veitch he found work with a builder at Niddrie, and was assured that every effort would be made to find a tenant or a buyer for the property. Some time later, he was informed by Mr. Veitch that a purchaser had been found, and after all expenses had been deducted from the sale he was left with a balance of only fifty pounds. With this and the remainder of the money which he received from the insurance of his father's vessel, he returned to Cromarty.

GOLF BALLS

A form of golf was being played on the links of Leith during the fifteenth century, and it is recorded that in 1459, James II ruled that the game was to be forbidden in Scotland, as it was interfering with archery practice, and other defensive activities. James IV, however, favoured a game of golf when time permitted, and Council accounts note that he had acquired clubs and balls for 'the playing at gowf at Leithe.' In those days, clubs and golf balls were expensive items, and at Banff Burgh Court there is even record of a boy who had stolen a ball, and was then 'ordainit' to be taken to the Gallowhill to be hanged on the gallows. These were the days of the 'feathery ball' where a hatful of feathers were stuffed into a leather cover, but there has been a huge advance in the manufacture of golf balls to tempt today's golfers, and we can now play with wound three piece, or solid two piece balls with natural or synthetic covers, and all with varying compression rates.

Leith has never really been known for the manufacture of golf balls, but in 1895, from a small office and workshop in Albert Street, the firm of J P Cochrane & Co., with a staff of six, produced the Rex and Paragon gutta ball, which were the first to be marketed by the Company. The owner, Mr Cochrane, was always looking to the future, and he experimented with a rubber-cored ball which earned the firm the reputation of having introduced the first of these balls, known as the Cochrane 'Bramble', which became popular with golfers during the early 1900's.

The Company began to grow, and as a result the premises in Albert Street were extended, and then a brick built factory on three floors was erected in Murano Place, and soon 180 employees were turning out some 30,000 balls each week. Business became so good that plans for a larger factory in Jameson Place were announced, where 700 workers would be employed with a projected output of 100,000 golf balls per week. Names such as the Ace, Professional, Professional Red Dot, Professional Yellow Dot and Liquid Core among others, began to make their way into the bags of golfers throughout this country, and many other parts of the golfing world.

The manufacturing process in the early days of the Cochrane golf ball went through several stages, the ball itself comprising two separate parts, namely the cover and the core. The gutta percha cover was made from the sap of certain trees found in Malaya and surrounding areas, and these were tapped to drain the sap off. After several processes, the gutta was rolled into thin sheets about six to eight inches wide, and of a creamy colour, and then hung to be dried and seasoned. The gutta gradually changed colour to black, and the strips were then rolled and cut into squares to the size and weight required for the cover of the golf ball. Some workers were involved in filling the little rubber inner bladders with liquid, and others would wind rubber tape into small balls before they were fed into machines to produce a balanced, weighted ball, of true dimensions. The covers were then manipulated by hand, and placed over the cores before being fed into steel moulds and taken to the cooling room to ensure that they kept their shape and size. The balls were then taken to the trimming shop, where any flaws were removed, and finally went to the paint department, where the paint was applied by rubbing on with the palm of the hand. When finished, they were stored in the drying room, and made ready for packing, boxing and despatching.

The head of the firm, Mr JP Cochrane, was the son of Mr John Cochrane, who was an ironmonger in the Kirkgate, and worked initially with Garland & Rodger, the timber merchants. Before opening his business as a golf ball manufacturer he was Manager of the Scottish Golf Club Manufacturing Company.

COUPER STREET SCHOOL

At the turn of the nineteenth century the Town Council of Leith devoted much of its energy to improving opportunities for local schooling. The school population had grown from 8,300 pupils to over 14,500 over a period of only three years and Couper Street School was one of several schools built in an attempt to cope with the increasing demand. The three-storey building, comprising 29 classrooms, staff rooms, cloakrooms and lavatories opened in 1890. The upper floor had a handsome timber glazed roof which was one of the features of an otherwise ordinary building.

The school drew its pupils from Junction Street School, South Fort Street School and St. Ninian's Hall in Commercial Street. The Infant Department opened in December 1890 with a school roll of 293, and an early report indicated that children being admitted were very backward and many had never been to school before. The Primary School opened on a temporary basis in St. Ninian's Hall in Commercial Street and when the main building was occupied there was a school roll of 1,426 which soon rose to 1,600. The log books of the day reported several outbreaks of scarlet fever, measles and mumps, and absenteeism and truancy were always a problem. Despite these problems, however, there were many happy times, and the School Sports were always well supported. These were held at Wardie Recreation Ground and crowds of around 1,200 were not unusual. Poverty and hardship were never far away, and in the depressed times of the thirties, needy children were issued with tickets for 'farthing breakfasts' which could be obtained from the Salvation Army and the local soup kitchen.

The day after the presentation of prizes in 1951, former headmasters and headmistresses revisited the school to say goodbye, and it closed on 29 June 1951. All that remains of the school are the red sandstone gate piers entering from Coburg Street and Admiralty Street and the stone built schoolhouse located in the south east corner of the site. Multi-storey flats now overlook the area where the school once stood amid the congested tenement blocks, but many Leithers will still have memories of their days at Couper Street School.

Couper Street School : Boarded up and awaiting demolition.

WHERE HAVE THEY GONE?

Over the past 150 years or so, Leith has witnessed a huge change in population, and where churches once stood, these have either been demolished or have been vacated and put to other use. The history of the churches in Leith is difficult to follow, and small groups seem to have continually splintered off to form other congregations, There were Seceders, Burghers and Antiburghers, Free Churches, United Presbyterian Churches and Relief Churches and indeed, it must have been something of a relief when in 1929, they all came together as the Presbytery of Edinburgh.

In South Leith there was Leith Kirkgate which seceded from South Leith Church in 1740, but it was not until 1775 that a new church was built in Coatfield Lane leading from the Kirkgate. This was rebuilt in 1792, but when a new church was built in Henderson Street in 1886, the old building was sold as a place of entertainment, and these in turn were destroyed by fire in 1888. The site was sold and became the Princess's Theatre, later to become the Gaiety Theatre, which was demolished as part of the redevelopment of the Kirkgate during the 1960s. Leith Kirkgate was said to have been located in an area where St. Anthony's Preceptory once stood, but with the union of this church with South Leith in 1973, Leith Kirkgate was demolished and new halls were built on the site.

Leith St. John's West once stood on the north side of Queen Charlotte Street and was demolished and the site sold for housing in 1964. Another Church which is often overlooked was located adjacent to St. James' Rectory in John's Place. It was built in 1844 but was burned down in 1880 and became the site for the building of a bonded warehouse which has now been converted into flats. This church was South Leith Free Church.

In North Leith, Leith St. Nicholas once occupied a site at the corner of Coburg Street and North Junction Street, and was built in 1844. An engraving on the outside wall of the building became known as the 'Burning Bush', and this feature was later built into St. Ninian's in Ferry Road when the congregations united in 1859. Leith St. Ninian's in Ferry Road was itself demolished in the 1980s to make way for a housing development and united with North Leith. Leith Harper Memorial Church was opened in Coburg Street in 1819 and was named after James Harper who served as minister from 1819 until 1864. The building was sold in 1963 and was later demolished to make way for a warehouse unit. Leith Bonnington occupied a site at the corner of Summerside Place and Summerside Street and was opened in 1880. The congregation joined with North Leith in 1968 and the site was developed for housing. The former St. Ninian's Church or the Mariners' Church, located in Commercial Street, took its name from the old St. Ninian's Chapel where the congregation of North Leith had worshipped before the move to Madeira Street. St. John's East, located in Constitution Street was closed in 1956 and was taken over by Edinburgh City Council, and St. Andrew's Church in Academy Street, the former St. Thomas' Church in Sheriff Brae and Dalmeny Street Church are now being used by other denominations.

Top - *The Shore : Panoramic view showing the former Leith Sailors' Home : Signal Tower : Former Maritime House : Housing development by Port of Leith Housing Association*

Middle - *The Shore : The Old Ship Hotel : Trade Winds Restaurant : Arched pend leading into Timber Bush*

Bottom - *The Shore : The King's Wark : Northern Mail Order Co. : Warehouse with crow stepped gable*

© Walter Taylor

Top -   The Shore : The former Seagull's Nest after restoration : The
        tenement block at the corner of Burgess Street : The gable of the
        former Unemployment Benefit Office

Middle - The Shore : Timber Bush

Bottom - The Cooperage : One of the first warehouses to be converted into
        flats inspired by The Leith Project

54

© Walter Taylor

© Walter Taylor

© Walter Taylor

Top -   Custom House Quay : The site where the first private housing
          development in Leith was located

Middle - Housing Development : Housing development by Heritage Homes
          with the Ocean Mist in the foreground

Bottom - Lamb's House : Built in the early years of the 17th century, the
          house is regarded as one of the finest merchant's houses in the City

© Walter Taylor

Top -   *Bangor Road : Looking towards Great Junction Street and the octagonal clock tower of the Leith Provident Co-operative Society building*

Middle - *Bowling Green Street : A wintry day looking towards the clock tower with the spire of the former St Thomas' Church in the background*

Bottom - *Ballantyne Road : Looking towards the State Picture House with the tenements awaiting demolition and redevelopment*

© Walter Taylor

© Walter Taylor

© Walter Taylor

PERSEVERE

1863

Top -   Leith Coat of Arms : South Leith Church Hall

Middle - The Provost's Chair : Leith Council Chamber

Bottom - The dry dock : Recess in the rear of a tenement building in Sandport
          Street to allow for the bowsprits of large sailing vessels using the dock

Top -   *The access to Timber Bush from The Shore with the site awaiting redevelopment by the Port of Leith Housing Association*

Middle - *Ronaldson's Wharf before sale and the clearance of the site for a modern flatted block*

Bottom - *The State, Leith's last cinema, closed in 1972 but continuing its use as a Bingo Hall*

Top -   *Decorative frieze : Leith Council*
           Chamber

Middle -   *The Lonely Leith Contractor*

Bottom -   *South Leith Church 1609-1909 :*
           Medal celebrating the tercentenary

Top -   *St. Ninian's Church, part of the Quayside Mills, showing the need for urgent repairs*

Middle-   *The Co-operative Society's site at Sheriff Brae, later to be developed as housing*

Bottom - *The former Northern Mail Order premises on The Shore with the Lawson Donaldson warehouse to the rear*

101 DATES IN LEITH

1128 The earliest reference to Inverleith in the charter of erection of the Abbey of Holyroodhouse founded by King David I

1329 King Robert I, Robert the Bruce, grants Edinburgh the right to the proceeds of all trade through the Port of Leith, with all other pertinents

1380 The Masters and Mariners of Leith granted by King Robert II the right to levy Prime Gilt on goods imported into Leith, this money to be used to relieve the sick, poor and aged

1398 Sir Robert Logan of Restalrig grants a wide ranging charter giving Edinburgh the liberty to erect wharves and quays, and access through the lands of Restalrig to the Port of Leith

1413 Sir Robert Logan of Restalrig grants a charter to Edinburgh conveying land for the storage of goods and merchandise carried to and from the Port

1423 King James I and his recently wedded English wife Joan Beaufort land at Leith

1430 The foundation of the Presbytery of St Anthony at Leith is confirmed by Bishop Wardlaw of St Andrews

1439 The earliest mention of a Leith shipbuilding family, the Corntons

1449 Mary of Gueldres, bride to be of James II lands at the King's Wark

1457 The earliest recorded evidence of golf in Scotland, when James II issues an instruction forbidding the playing of golf as it interfered with archery and other defence activities

1483 The building of the great kirk of St Mary's on the site where South Leith Parish Church now stands

1486 Robert Ballantyne, Abbot of Holyrood builds first bridge over the river connecting South Leith to North Leith. Records indicate that there may have been a bridge as early as 1400

1493 The chapel of St Ninian founded at the North end of Robert Ballantyne's bridge

1497 The Plague visits Leith

1505 The Margaret, the first ship of James IV's fleet in Scotland is launched at Leith

1512 The Great Michael is launched at Newhaven

1537 James V and Queen Magdalene land at Leith where she kneels, kisses the ground and prays to God to bless the people

1544 The Earl of Hertford and his army land at Leith with orders to 'sack Leith, burn and subject it, and put man, woman and child to fire and sword'

1549 Leith garrisoned by French troops

1555 The Kirkmasters of Leith acquire a piece of land for the building of a Fraternity House

1555 The superiority of the town purchased by the Queen Regent on behalf of Mary, Queen of Scots from Sir Robert Logan of Restalrig

1559 Fortifications around Leith built and strengthened by the French

1560 Leith besieged by the English Army

1560 Mary of Guise dies and fortifications around Leith ordered to be removed. French troops withdraw

1561 Mary, Queen of Scots lands at Leith and stays briefly at Andrew Lamb's house before being conveyed to Holyrood Palace

1565 Mary, Queen of Scots mortgages the superiority of Leith to Edinburgh in consideration of money advanced by the community of the City

1577 The Duke of Lennox, Regent and his lieutenant the Earl of Morton establish headquarters in Leith and form a Council Chamber on the Coalhill

1592 The Town Council of Edinburgh passes by-laws forbidding golf on Sundays. It was known that John Knox enjoyed a game in the afternoon when his duties in the pulpit were ended

1616 King James VI grants a patent to permit whaling from Leith

1631 Newhaven annexed to the Parish of North Leith

1638 Solemn League and Covenant signed on Leith Links and again in 1643

1642 King Charles I is engaged in a game of golf on Leith Links when he is told of the Irish Rebellion

1645 The last visit of bubonic plague to Leith causing 2736 deaths out of a population of 4000

1649 The Edinburgh Council builds a Weigh House on the site of the old tennis court in the King's Wark

1650 King Charles II visits his troops on Leith Links and stays for a time in the mansion of Lord Balmerino in the Kirkgate

1655 General Monk starts work on the building of the Citadel at a cost of £100,000

1661 Earliest reference to horse racing in 'Mercurius Caledonius'

1663 Glassmaking starts in a glasshouse near the Citadel

1698 The Endeavour, Caledonia, St Andrew and Unicorn sail from Leith Roads with 1200 settlers as part of the Darien Expedition

1709 Edinburgh Town Council presents a silver arrow to the Company of Archers for annual competition on Leith Links

1720 First dry dock in Scotland opens in Leith but date disputed

1744 The Honourable Edinburgh Company of Golfers is formed, and draws up first written rules of golf

1750 The Edinburgh Whale Fishing Company is established

1754 The Rules of the Gentlemen Golfers adopted by the accredited home of golf at St Andrews

1763 Stage Coach service between Edinburgh and Leith takes one hour to complete the journey

1779 Paul Jones arrives off Leith on board 'Le Bonne Homme Richard'

1780 Leith Fort under construction to a design by James Craig, planner of the new town

1789 Robert Ballantyne's bridge over the river replaced by a drawbridge

1793 Leith Banking Company established

1806 First wet dock opened in Leith

1809 A Martello Tower is built on Mussel Cape Rocks at a cost of £17,000. It is built as part of a scheme to defend Edinburgh against attacks by the French during the Napoleonic wars

1812 Leith Custom House is built at the Sandport

1816 Leith Races move to Musselburgh

1818 Junction Bridge is built to continue Great Junction Street from Foot of Leith Walk to the western end of the new docks

1821 The Trinity Chain Pier is constructed by Captain Samuel Brown of the Royal Navy at a cost of £4,000

1822 George IV lands at Leith, the first visit of a British monarch to Scotland since Charles I

1822 The last execution takes place in Leith from a gibbet placed near to the foot of Constitution Street

1827 The Third Police Act defines the boundaries of Leith for the first time

1829 Mons Meg, the huge 17th century cannon captured by the English is returned from the Tower of London to Edinburgh by sea through Leith

1833 Leith gains independence from Edinburgh and elects Adam Whyte as first Provost

1837 Menzies & Co launch the PS Sirius from their yard near the Old Dock gates. This passenger ship was the first steamship to sail the East to West Atlantic crossing entirely under her own steam

1838 Scotland's first passenger rail service opens in South Leith operating horse drawn cars

1839 The Mariners' Church in Commercial Street built

1840 Leith Chamber of Commerce founded

1846 Restrictions on trade are ended by the Burgh Trading Act

1851 Leith Hospital opens

1852 The Victoria Dock is built at a cost of £200,000 to a design by James Rendel

1855 Leith Navigation School opens in The Mariners' Church in Commercial Street

1856 Leith Town Council acquires Leith Links from Edinburgh

1869 The Albert Dock is built at a cost of £300,000, and is opened by Provost Watt

1871 The first tramway service commences from Bernard Street to Haymarket

1873 Leith Hospital is extended

1874 The Victoria Swing Bridge is completed. At the time it was the largest swing bridge in the United Kingdom

1883 Leith Sailor's Home is built on land granted by Leith Dock Commission. Converted into an hotel in 1994

1903 Leith Central Station is opened by the North British Railway

1903 Leith Nautical College opens in Commercial Street, the first college of its kind in Scotland

1905 Electric tram car service commences in Leith

1914 The Glitra becomes the first Leith ship to be sunk during the war when, bound from Grangemouth to Stavanger she is stopped and sunk by a German U-boat

1915 214 officers and men of the 1:7 Battalion the Royal Scots, mainly Leith volunteers, are killed in a rail disaster at Quintinshill near Gretna on their way to the Dardanelles

1916 Leith suffers minor damage as the result of a German Zeppelin raid

1920 Leith amalgamates with Edinburgh under an Act of Parliament. Provost John Lindsay presides over the last Town Council

1928 The Leith-built sailing ship 'Kobenhavn' lost in the South Atlantic with 60 lives

1939 Leith suffers the first air raid of the war when German bombers attack the Forth

1940 HMS Cossack lands prisoners of war from the captured German ship 'Altmark'

1942 Work on the Western break-water in the docks is completed and opened by Rt Hon Tom Johnstone, Secretary of State for Scotland

1944 13 pier heads are built and launched from Leith as part of the Mulberry Harbour used for the D-Day landings

1950 A licence is granted for a seaplane service from Leith but withdrawn in 1959 due to lack of support.

1956 The Queen and the Duke of
Edinburgh arrive in Leith aboard
the Royal Yacht Britannia at
the start of a three day visit to
Edinburgh

1958 The opening of deep water facilities
at Leith Docks

1960 The demolition and rebuilding of
the old Kirkgate

1961 Andrew Lamb's house is converted
into a day centre for the elderly

1967 Leith Dock Commission is wound
up and becomes the Forth Ports
Authority

1969 New entrance lock is officially
opened by HRH Prince Philip, Duke
of Edinburgh

1976 Port of Leith Housing Association
is formed

1980 Leith Project commences

1984 Henry Robb's shipyard closes

1992 Leith Docks is privatised and
becomes Forth Ports plc

1994 New Scottish Office building under
construction. Queen Margaret
College create new campus in
former Leith Academy Secondary
School

1995 Cutty Sark Tall Ships Race starts
from Leith

1999 Following her decommisioning
the former Royal Yacht Britannia
is permanently berthed in the
Western Harbour

2001 Ocean Terminal opens creating a
large shopping mall and visiting
centre for the former Royal Yacht
berthed nearby

THE PORT OF LEITH

Sir, the parallel between the relations of Leith with Edinburgh and those of Scotland with England are possibly closer than some local observers have observed.

Certain clauses of the Treaty of Union of 1710 contained concessions and guarantees made to the Scots as a condition of their entering into partnership with England, and it is common knowledge that a number of those clauses have been violated. So, in 1920, the Act of Parliament extending the boundaries of Edinburgh to include Leith, laid on Edinburgh certain obligations which represented concessions to Leith.

One of them was the provision of a new Town Hall, the sad story of which is well known. Another, was the provision of bathing facilities between Newhaven and Granton.

Instead of making such provision, the Corporation laid a main sewer at this point, and has grossly neglected the sea front both there and elsewhere. Yet another was the provision of a large public park with facilities for football: instead of making such provision, the Corporation removed the prohibition of football from Leith Links, which, with its light, sandy soil is totally unfit for football, and may have suffered serious consequences as a result.

Must we conclude that Edinburgh, like England, has not kept faith, and that Leith, like Scotland, was enticed into a union under a misapprehension as to the sanctity of the instrument of incorporation? It is at any rate plain that the Act of 1920 is worthy of attention.

Gordon Donaldson, Leith

Top -   *Boatyard : Looking up-river from Junction Bridge towards boatyard and slipway*

Middle -   *Bonnington Road : Looking from Great Junction Street down Bonnington Road with Burlington Street on the right*

Bottom -   *Burlington Street : Looking along Burlington Street with arched opening engraved Leith Provident Co-operative Society on tenement building*

Top - *Burlington Street : Burlington Street after demolition giving temporary home for the Circus Hoffman*

Middle - *Bonnington Road : Bonnington Road with Tennant Street on the left and Bonnington Road School in the distance*

Bottom - *Manderston Street : Looking from Leith Walk towards Easter Road*

Top - *Kirkgate Shopping Centre : A rest from shopping at the new shopping centre with buildings due to be demolished in the background*

Middle - *Duke Street : Looking along Duke Street towards the Foot of Leith Walk. The site stands empty awaiting redevelopment*

Bottom - *The Buttercup : A fire at the Buttercup at the foot of Easter Road*

Top -   *Site works underway prior to the rebuilding of Wishart's warehouse*
Middle - *The site of the former dry dock adjoining Ronaldson's Wharf*
Bottom - *The dilapidated tenements in Coburg Street awaiting refurbishment*

Top -   *Buchanan Street : The tenements of Buchanan Street looking
           towards Iona Street*

Middle - *Boundary Square : The new Buchanan Street*

Bottom - *Chancelot Flour Mills : The flour mills of the Scottish Co-operative
           Wholesale Society Ltd. awaiting demolition*

Top -   The Foot of Leith Walk : A quiet Sunday morning
Middle -   Queen Charlotte Street: Lodge No. 5
Bottom - Memorial Stone : The Leith Improvement Scheme of 1885

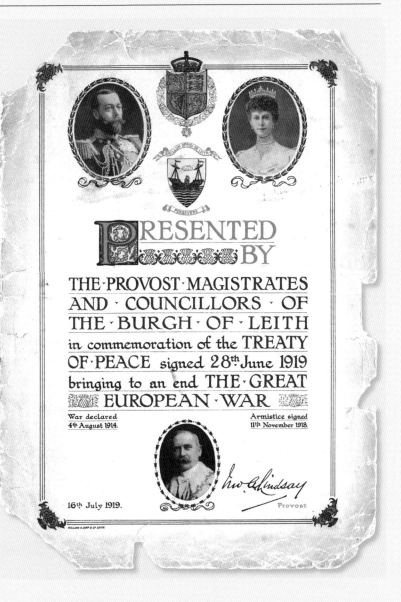

The Certificate presented by the magistrates and councillors to the citizens of Leith to commemorate the ending of the Great War, 1919

Top -   Ornate ceiling :
         Leith Council Chamber

Middle - Golf on Leith Links : A foursome
         in progress with Wellington Place
         and St. James' Church in the background.

Bottom - Plaques : Commemorating Leith Links as the historical home of the
         Honourable Company of Edinburgh Golfers

72

FANCY THAT

A national golf match among the professionals of the day took place over Leith Links on 17 May 1867, and among those taking part were Old Tom and Young Tom Morris, J Anderson and R Kirk of St Andrews, Willie Park, David Park, R Hunter, Tom Brown and R Ferguson of Musselburgh, and Willie Dunn of Leith. The course at that time was of seven holes, and four rounds were played, the winner being R Ferguson of Musselburgh who returned a score of 131. The tournament, which had been organised by Leith Thistle Golf Club, carried a total prize fund of £25.

A REMARKABLE TALE

King James VI of Scotland and I of England paid only one visit to Scotland after the Union of the Crowns, but during this visit a quantity of silver plate and other goods went missing, and were never recovered. Two hundred and seventy-seven years later, the session of South Leith Church thought it desirable to obtain two further communion cups to serve the growing congregation,

and Dr. James Mitchell, then first charge, presented a cup to the session which he had obtained during a visit to Hamburg. Dr. Mitchell had a duplicate made to provide a matching pair, but on returning to Hamburg shortly afterwards, he found the neighbour to the first cup in an antique dealer's shop and purchased it. He then exchanged this cup for the duplicate which he himself had presented to the kirk session.

Communion Cups : The cups bear the Royal Arms of England and are dated 1617

The cups bear the Royal Arms of England, and are dated 1617, and bear the inscription, 'Beati Pacifici.' which means, 'Blessed are the Peacemakers.' It is thought that these were the cups that King James brought to Scotland during his visit in 1617, and which were among the goods lost from his possessions.

The King's association with South Leith Church was well known, and preparations for his visit were being made with the building of the King's Loft, but if the story was true that the cups had indeed been lost, rediscovered in unusual circumstances, and returned almost three centuries later, then this must be the most remarkable of all stories to be told about Leith.

GAIETY THEATRE

Conversation about Leith will inevitably lead to reminiscing about the old Kirkgate, and the Gaiety Theatre which played such an important part in the community life of Leith until they were demolished in the sixties, as part of the comprehensive development of the area.

The early days of the theatre are a little obscure, but records do show that in the 1880s, a music hall of sorts was housed in a hall adjoining the Old Kirkgate United Presbyterian Church, the acts being promoted by H E Moss, who at that time owned the Gaiety in Chambers Street, Edinburgh.

© Walter Taylor

The Gaiety Theatre : 'The good old days' gone forever

The Old Kirkgate UP Church which was located between the Kirkgate and Coatfield Lane was built in 1775, and could seat some 1,050 persons. It was rebuilt in 1801, reseated in 1829, and prior to the move to Henderson Street, had been used as a place of worship for one hundred and eleven years. The congregation decided to move to a new site, however, and the new church in Henderson Street was opened in October 1886. A buyer for the original building had been difficult to find, but it was eventually purchased by a Mr Edward Edgar, together with several adjoining properties for a price of £1,500. Later, Mr Edgar leased the hall for a term to a company of music hall artists, who found that its interior arrangements were not suited to the nature of their performances, and an application was made to Leith Dean of Guild Court to have the building altered and improved, in order to receive a licence for future performances. The Court, however, required certain alterations to be made which were of a substantial nature, and the owner deemed it necessary to defer the scheme.

During the evening of March 2 1888, a fire broke out which completely destroyed the property, and so fierce were the flames that at one time it was thought that burning embers would endanger the roof of South Leith Church. In 1889, the owner, Mr Edgar, leased the burnt-out site to Mr H E Moss, who built a new theatre which was called the Princess' Theatre, and Mr Frederick Wright took over as Director/Manager. The new theatre could accommodate one thousand people in the pit and gallery, and the Grand Opening took place with a play called 'False Nights'. The artistes for this play were transported by horse cab to the Princess' Theatre from the Gaiety in Chambers Street. The theatre was reconstructed in 1899 under the name of the New Gaiety Theatre.

On January 8 1900, the installation of full electric lighting to the theatre took place, and the programme included The Monster Variety Company, with Miss Kate Devere, Impersonator, and the celebrated Valentine Bennion Anglo American Marionettes. The Chalmer's Cinematograph also showed pictures of the war in the Transvaal, the first occasion that cinema was shown at the theatre. In 1913, further alterations to the theatre took place, and shops on either side of the main entrance were acquired allowing access to the gallery, circle and pit from the Kirkgate entrance, without the need for waiting outside for the second house. The Gaiety had now become better known as a picture house, but with the departure of Mr Tabel to become Manager of the Palace Picture House in July 1944, live theatre returned to the Gaiety with Will Fyffe, Tommy Hope and the 8 Calder Sisters.

In 1946, Mr Claude Worth managed the Gaiety on behalf of the proprietors who were registered as 'Leith Entertainments Ltd.', and for the next ten years, programmes alternated between pictures and live theatre. The last show was performed on August 22 1955 with 'Laugh of a Lifetime', featuring Tommy Loman, Johnny Beattie and the four Kordites.

The Gaiety became the victim of slum clearance in the Kirkgate, but during its relatively short life, the management and players had provided a splendid location for amusement for the local community.

GIBSON BIPLANE

During the early 1900s, Mr. John Gibson was designing biplanes in Leith, which were built by the Caledonian Cycle Company at an address at 109 Leith Walk, adjoining the railway arches. These aeroplanes were known as the Gibson Biplane No. 1, which was built in 1909, and the Gibson Biplane No. 2, which was a modified version of the original design which was built a year later.

Technically, the aeroplanes were single seat 'pusher' biplanes, powered by a two cylinder horizontally-opposed 30 horse power Alvaston engine, with radiators mounted vertically behind the pilot. The modified version, the No. 2, had the same power unit, but the frame differed in several respects. A biplane fore elevator was used in place of the earlier monoplane type, and extended skids were used to give additional support. The original monoplane rudder was also replaced by biplane surfaces, and some alteration was made to the undercarriage struts. Flight Magazine of 1910 refers to this Scottish built biplane, and to the designer's comments as follows: 'The machine which we are at present practising with promises well, and rises steadily, but none of us are capable of handling her efficiently as yet. Of course, we have had our engine troubles and

The Gibson Biplane : The first Scottish-built aeroplane to leave the ground

a few smashes, but all the faults are either with the engine, or with our own inexperienced handling, which time will remedy. The machine itself is alright, and I believe it is the first Scottish-built aeroplane to leave the ground. My son, aged 19 can handle her best.'

One of the biplanes was exhibited in the Aeronautical Hall at the Glasgow International Exhibition in 1911, but the firm was never able to expand into full production due to preferential subsidies going to larger firms during the First World War.

THE EXPERIMENT

A paddle ship designed by Patrick Miller of Dalswinton was launched from the yard of Allan and Stewart in Leith in 1788, and was the forerunner of the paddle steamer. Of unconventional design, she had wheels which could be used for moving in calm conditions, but she was regarded as being ungainly in her sailing habits.

GLASS MAKING

Glass making is said to have been introduced into Leith during the 1660s, when a glasshouse was built in the vicinity of the Citadel. The business was started by Robert Pape, but it did not prosper, as glassmakers from Newcastle and London were concerned at the introduction of this new business into Scotland. They began to flood the market with their own glass in order to stifle the growth of the trade, and this action eventually forced a closure.

A new attempt to establish a glasshouse was made in 1678, when Sir James Stanfield, and four other partners enticed skilled workers from Newcastle to Leith in order to train local men in this highly skilled trade. The work produced was of a poor quality, however, and the Citadel glasshouse closed in 1681, and was put up for sale. The buyers were Sir James Stanfield and Sir Robert Gordon, and Alexander Ainslie was appointed as manager. Skilled workers were brought from Newcastle, but again, the business did not seem to prosper.

However, Ainslie, and three other business partners tried once again to develop the business, and this time concentrated on bottle making, and at last the Leith Glass Company managed to survive. The works at the Citadel under Ainslie were eventually sold in 1728, but after several other transactions had taken place, a fire destroyed the buildings in 1747, and glassmaking at the Citadel came to an end. However, one of the former owners, Robert Wightman, with others, moved to a leased site on the sands of South Leith, and built the first glasshouse there.

The business was then known as the Edinburgh Glasshouse Co., but those in Leith knew it as the Bottlehouse Company, as it was the manufacture of bottles which the business specialised in. Business was so good that an adjoining piece of ground was feued, and a second cone was built, and began to produce in 1764. Due to the wine trade, the manufacture of green bottles was the main output during the earlier years, but as the business expanded, white bottles were produced. Soon, a third and fourth cone were built, allowing flint glass and window glass to be added to the output.

A second company, called the Leith Glasshouse Company was established in 1790, and soon seven cones were working flat out on the site now bordering the north line of the present Salamander Street. Despite the eventual success of Leith's glassmaking business after a difficult start during the 1660s, taxation was to become the burden which eventually put an end to the manufacture of glass in the area. The Edinburgh Glasshouse Co. had gone out of business, and was advertised for sale in the Courant of 1813 at a value of £40,000, together with a sixteen horse power steam engine valued at £21,000. The Leith Glasshouse Co. managed to survive for a few years, operating with only two cones, and although the tax burden was reduced in 1825, it was too late to save the Company, and it too went out of business.

Salamander Street is now the only reference which remains of Leith's part in the glass making industry, the salamander being a fire proof lizard of medieval legend, which was likened to the fire and smoke which belched from the brick-built cones which once stood on the site.

IN REMEMBRANCE

Dr. Johnston came to Leith from Langton in Dumfriesshire in 1765, and for fifty-nine years he held the charge of North Leith, becoming one of the most respected figures in Edinburgh during this time. He saw his parish grow from a small hamlet into a thriving township, and devoted himself to helping children, the poor and the handicapped. He was also grateful for the assistance which was given to him by John Gladstones, who became Session Clerk, and his elder brother James, who later became Treasurer, and they all became good friends.

David Johnston received his Doctorate from Edinburgh University in 1781, and in 1793 he established an Asylum for the industrious blind in Edinburgh which became the forerunner of the Royal Blind Asylum and School. He kept trying to improve the conditions of the poor, and established a school for children, and a music school. As North Leith grew, it became apparent that the church was becoming too small for the increase in population, and a search was made for a new site, which was eventually found in Madeira Street.

The foundation stone was laid in 1814, and the fine new church opened in 1816. At this stage, Dr. Johnston retired, but occasionally preached, and still made regular visits throughout the parish. In 1812, he made the long journey to London by stagecoach in order to baptise a grandchild, and when there, he was informed that he was to be made a knight. However, the eminent person who was to confer the honour had to cancel the presentation, and it was postponed for two weeks. Dr. Johnston refused to wait, and he returned home, and was never to become Sir David. After his retirement, he became a rather lonely figure, and he died in 1824 at the age of ninety. The funeral to North Leith Burial Ground was attended by some five hundred people, and the path to his resting place was lined by the men and boys from the Asylum for the Industrious Blind.

The session minute of the time reads, *'Never was a Pastor more beloved by his Flock; Never a Pastor more deserving of a People's affection and esteem'.*

Thomas Gladstones was a flour and barley merchant in the Coalhill, and came from land owning stock in the West of Scotland. He married Helen Neilson, and in 1764, their son John was born, a son who was to become the father of William Ewart Gladstone, the great Liberal Prime Minister.

John Gladstones moved to Liverpool where for over 50 years he was to rank as one of the most successful businessmen of his day, and accumulated great wealth, much of which he donated to the church and other good causes. In 1835, he obtained license to drop the final 's' in his surname, and from then on he became known as John Gladstone. He was influenced into politics, and became the Member for Lancaster, then Woodstock and finally Berwick in 1827. In 1846, he was created a baronet, and died at his home at Fasque near Fettercairn in 1851, aged 87. In 1840, Sir John Gladstone, Bart., erected the former St. Thomas' Church, together with the manse, schoolhouse, rose garden and womens' asylum in Mill Lane.

The tomb containing the remains of Thomas Gladstones and his wife Helen Neilson, parents of Sir John, and grandparents of William Ewart Gladstone can still be seen in North Leith Burial Ground.

Anne Farquharson was born in 1723, the daughter of John Farquharson of Invercauld, and his third wife Margaret, daughter of Lord James Murray. She married Aeneas Mackintosh of Mackintosh in 1741 when she was only eighteen, and spent her early years at Moy Hall during the turbulent times in the Highlands, and the rise of Jacobitism. She mobilised the Mackintosh clan in support of Prince Charles, and was often depicted as a large lady mounted on a white horse at the head of her regiment, but this description was more fanciful than fact. She earned the respect of the Jacobite army, and came to be known as 'Colonel Anne' during the uprising.

Throughout her life, she defended her part in supporting Prince Charles during the spring of 1746, and she was elected a burgess freewoman and guildsister of Inverness in 1763. She had no children, and survived her husband by some fourteen years. She died in Leith on 2 March 1784 after a short illness, and was interred in North Leith Burial Ground beside other members of the family of Farquharson of Invercauld.

The Haven. If you have ever been to Coldingham Bay near St Abbs, you may have seen the hotel called The Haven perched high on the cliffs overlooking the sea. What has this to do with Leith you may ask? Well, the original house was built by Miss Jane Hay of Leith in 1905, and was also used by her as an office. Jane was a very much respected lady in the area, and she was a close friend of Mrs Kennedy Fraser the composer, who frequently visited her. She was very fond of children, and gave a home to many orphans at The Haven, and it is said that the father of the last child to be given shelter there was drowned, when the *Titanic* sank in the Atlantic. She also organised dancing classes in the village hall, and gave instruction in several subjects from her home, but Jane Hay will perhaps best be remembered for her work in connection with the local lifeboat, as she was largely responsible for the first lifeboat being located at St Abbs.

The Alfred Erlandsen had foundered off shore in 1907 with the loss of all hands, and seeing the urgent need for a lifeboat in the area, she persevered with her efforts until her wishes were realised. Jane Hay died in France in 1914, and her body was brought home and laid to rest in the churchyard at Coldingham, and in St Abb's Church there is a plaque to the memory of this Leith lady in recognition of her work on behalf of the community and lifeboat men.

John Home. John Home was born in 1724 in a house on the east side of what is now called Maritime Street, near to the junction with Bernard Street. His father was Town Clerk, and after schooling at the Grammar School in the Kirkgate, he went to Edinburgh University to study for the ministry, but after becoming licensed by the Presbytery, he abandoned his chosen vocation, and as a volunteer, became involved in the defence of Edinburgh against Prince Charles Edward.

Whilst serving in the Hanoverian interest, he was taken prisoner and held at the castle of Doune, from where he escaped, and eventually landed back in Leith on board the sloop *Vulture*. He became associated with the eminent literati of Edinburgh, and was inducted as minister at Athelstaneford. He turned his talents to writing, and in 1755, he completed the tragedy '*Douglas*', but it was rejected by Garrick in London, who deemed it unsuitable for the stage. The work was received with more enthusiasm in Edinburgh, but it never managed to achieve the acclaim which Home thought it deserved, although it was performed at the Edinburgh Festival in 1950. He resigned from the church and published other works, and in 1763, he was appointed Conservator of Scottish Privileges. His last tragedy '*Alfred*', was published in 1802, and in his eighty-fourth year, John Home died and was buried in South Leith churchyard.

A GREAT OCCASION

The landing of King George IV at Leith in 1822 is considered to be one of the great occasions in Leith's history, and a fine painting of the event still hangs in the Old Council Chamber in Leith. The landing might not have taken place at Leith at all as there were some who thought that the Chain Pier at Trinity would be a more suitable landing point, but a petition supporting the landing at Leith was sent to the King who granted permission to land at The Shore. When the Royal Squadron arrived in Leith Roads it was very wet, and it was agreed that the King would not land until midday on the following day. A few minutes before twelve o' clock on that day, the King embarked on the Royal barge, accompanied by all his dignitaries, and he was received on The Shore by the Port Admiral, the Lord Provost and Magistrates of Leith, and many others including Sir Walter Scott. He received a tremendous welcome as he made his way to the Royal carriage, and his landing is commemorated by a plate on the quayside bearing an inscription in Latin meaning O Happy Day. He was the first reigning monarch to have set foot in Scotland for almost 200 years.

© Walter Taylor

A Great Occasion : The commemorative plaque on the quay wall indicating where George IV landed in 1822

THE TERRACES

When we speak of the Colonies we usually think of the terraces at Stockbridge, but these early housing developments were also built in Leith from the middle of the nineteenth century. There was a groundswell of opinion that not enough was being done to improve housing conditions at that time, and led by several campaigners, including Hugh Miller, the Edinburgh Co-operative Building Company was formed with a beehive as its emblem.

The first project was undertaken at Stockbridge, and so successful was this development that a small site was purchased in Leith at Hawthornbank, off North Fort Street, where forty-four houses were built along similar lines to those that had been erected at Stockbridge. Many of these houses were purchased or rented by people who were locally employed in Leith. This early encouragement, however did not last long, as a site which had been developed in Ferry Road took almost three years to sell and this seriously affected the financing of future developments. Further land was eventually purchased at Restalrig Park, and the houses that were built there were referred to as the 'high terraces' and were said to have been named after the shrubs and trees which had once grown over the area. The first terrace, built around 1868 was called Woodbine Terrace, followed by Woodville, Thornville, Ashville, Beechwood, Elmwood and finally Oakwood Terrace in 1883. An engraved stone commemorating the work undertaken by the building company at Restalrig Park can still be seen.

The last Edinburgh Co-operative Building Company development in Leith was also built at Restalrig Park, but the original layouts were improved. The houses now had a bay window and access was made by means of an internal passage and stair. These developments were undertaken around the turn of the century and included the Ryehills, Cornhill Terrace, East Restalrig Terrace, and several of the older type houses in Restalrig Road and Summerfield Place.

A similar type of house was also being built in Leith towards the end of the nineteenth century by the Industrial Co-operative Building Company. These were referred to as the 'low terraces,' and were built on ground once occupied by Hermitage House. East Hermitage Place and Rosevale Terrace were completed but the Company ran out of funds, and was finally wound up in 1875. A local builder, A & W Fingzies demolished the main house and completed the remainder of the terraces. The former Hermitage Terrace was renamed Rosevale Terrace in 1968, Livingstone Place is now called Somerset Place and Waverley Place was renamed Lindean Place in 1969. Cochrane Place was named after the former owner of Hermitage House, Fingzies Place after the builder, and Noble Place was named after Grace Noble who was his wife.

THE GORDON HIGHLANDER

Corporal W Orr once lived in Drum Terrace, Leith, and joined the 13th Battalion the Gordon Highlanders in 1916. He was in a reserved occupation at the outbreak of the First World War, and was an older man with a family to take care of. Feelings had been running high in the country after the casualties which had been suffered on the Somme and at Passchendaele, and those men who were not in the forces became a target for abuse. To protect them, the Government brought out the Derby Scheme, and armbands were worn to indicate that they were willing to volunteer for the Front if required.

The 13th Battalion the Gordon Highlanders had taken many casualties and there was great reluctance among replacements to join the Battalion because of the superstition attached to it. Men were therefore asked to volunteer to serve in this unit, and Corporal Orr took the view that if he was to be killed in action it didn't matter whether he was in the 13th Battalion or not.

He did his training at Edinburgh Castle, and then went to France where he was engaged in the push at Etappe, but he was later returned to Liverpool Hospital with trench foot which was a common complaint caused by standing for lengths of time in waterlogged trenches. He was due to return to France after his discharge from hospital, but was thankful that the War had ended before he could return to the Front. He recalled that he had another Leith man as a friend who served with him but during an advance he was caught by an exploding shell and was not seen again. He also recalled that when in Liverpool Hospital, a Welsh Captain was admitted to have a leg amputated. Blood transfusions were largely unknown at that time, and he volunteered to give blood. He and the Captain lay side by side while his blood was transferred through a tube directly to the Captain who made a good recovery and afterwards shared his whisky ration with the gallant Scot.

Whatever memories Corporal Orr may have had during his experiences in the war, he was immensely proud to have served in the 13th Battalion, and his papers, Derby armband and his kilt were later gifted to the Army Museum in Edinburgh Castle by his family.

STRANGE SMELLS

At a meeting of the Public Health Committee in 1901, Treasurer Craig complained about smells coming from Salamander Street which, with the wind blowing from the east were said to be affecting houses in Gladstone Place, and tarnishing silver and brass items in the rooms. Bailie Manclark supported the complaint, and said that he had developed a sore throat on three occasions as a result of these strong odours. The Provost admitted that he himself had never been affected by these smells, and suggested that a fuss was being made out of nothing. "*I wish there were more of them,*" he said. "*Doesn't Leith prosper as a result of these smells?*" The matter was dropped.

HARBOUR AND DOCKS

The harbour of Leith was formed where the Water of Leith flowed into the Firth of Forth, and was tidal until 1969. There was a sandbar too, which lay across the mouth of the river, and the effect of the tides and the sand bar made access to the harbour difficult at times. In order to divert the currents, lines of piers were constructed, but due to the strong easterly winds which constantly blew, it reached a point when vessels could scarcely pass in or out.

The first pier, constructed of wood, was burned down in 1544, but some years later another wooden pier was built and used for 240 years until the last traces disappeared around 1850. In 1710 a stone pier was built as an extension to the wooden pier, and this appeared to reduce the effects of the tides and sandbar. In 1753 an Act was passed for enlarging and deepening the harbour, but funding could not be raised, and as a result nothing was done. Soon after this, another scheme was put forward which required the formation of a canal leading to a deep water basin, but this too was abandoned. In 1777, a short pier was built on the west side of the harbour, and became known as the Custom House Quay.

In 1799 John Rennie, an engineer, presented proposals for a new dock, and in 1788 an Act of Parliament gave the Magistrates of Edinburgh power to borrow £30,000 in order to improve the harbour facilities. A plan by Robert Whitworth,

© Walter Taylor

*The Harbour and Docks : A ship passing through the lock gates
before entering the Firth of Forth*

an engineer, was abandoned, and the Magistrates of Edinburgh again applied
to Parliament for increased borrowing which was authorised at £160,000, to
enable some of the proposals previously made by John Rennie to be carried
out. On the 14 May 1801 the foundation stone of the new East Dock was laid,
and in 1806 the dock was opened to shipping. The West, or Queen's Dock which
commenced building in 1810, was completed in 1817 at a cost of £285,000. In
1825 the City of Edinburgh borrowed further funds of £240,000 on the security
of the dock dues. Mr Chapman of Newcastle carried out surveys, and prepared
plans for further improvements, and as a result of this, the eastern pier was
extended and a western pier and breakwater were built.

At this time Edinburgh was insolvent, and in order to manage the increasing
trade of the Port, an Act of Parliament was passed in 1838, enabling control
to be vested in eleven Commissioners. In 1847 another government grant was
raised for the building of a new dock, and the Victoria Dock as it was known was
opened in 1852, further enlarging the existing accommodation for vessels.

The Harbour and Docks Bill was passed by the House of Lords in 1860, and
this effectively cancelled the debt of £230,000 due to the Treasury under a
cancellation fee of £50,000. By 1862, with a further increase in trade, Messrs
Rendell and Robertson, civil engineers, were instructed to prepare plans
to reclaim land on the east side of the river, and in 1869 the Albert Dock
was completed at a cost of £224,500, including all cranage and sheds on the
quayside. This dock was almost twice the size of those constructed on the
western side of the harbour, and was connected to them by the Victoria Swing
Bridge. Dry dock accommodation was also considered, and the Prince of Wales's
Graving Dock was opened in 1858. The formation of the Edinburgh Dock was a
huge undertaking, as a strong sea wall was built, land reclaimed, and pumping
machinery installed in purpose-built buildings near to the dock gates. The
opening took place in 1881 before a huge crowd estimated at around 80,000.
The last dock to be built was the Imperial Dock, the largest in the Port, which
was opened in 1903. In 1942, the east and west breakwaters were substantially
improved, and further work was carried out at the Western Harbour.

LEITH AXE

The Leith Axe, which was first recorded in 1521, was described as a long shafted weapon with a two-edged axe blade, and a hook projecting from the end of the shaft. It was similar to the French halberd, and was apparently made in Leith and used during the first half of the sixteenth century.

LIGHTNING PLEBISCITE

The Reform Bill of 1833 gave Leith its independence from Edinburgh, and the Port began to bustle with activity. Industry started to expand, jobs were created, Port trade increased, and Leith businesses large and small began to flourish. Four hundred men left Leith by train each day to work on the building of the Forth Rail Bridge. Municipal buildings, reflecting the Victorian age and Leith's new independent status, began to change the face of the town. Public services such as transport, police and fire were developed, and Leithers were proud of their superior electric tramway system, which was not compatible with the cable cars of Edinburgh. Changing between the two systems became known as the 'Pilrig Muddle,' and Leithers on the way 'up town' to Edinburgh would say with some relish, *"if ye're in a hurry, get aff at Pilrig and walk the rest."*

Meanwhile, Edinburgh had continued its expansion of boundaries, and in 1894 a Memorandum from the Town Clerk of Edinburgh requested some discussion on possible amalgamation, but this was rejected. By 1896, however, Edinburgh had acquired a further 2,468 acres of land on the western and southern fringes of the City, including Portobello, leaving Leith effectively surrounded.

*Leith for Ever : A banner protesting against the amalgamation
with the City of Edinburgh in 1920*

Further pressures on amalgamation were delayed by the First World War, but by 1918 another Extension Bill was prepared by Edinburgh. Leith Town Council refused to give assent to any Bill, and the issue finally came to a head in January 1920, when, at a meeting of the Council, it was decided to adopt the suggestion of a plebiscite which had been reported in an Editorial in the Leith Observer. The Edinburgh Evening News referred to this turn of events as 'the Lightning Plebiscite,' because of the speed at which the arrangements for the poll had been conducted. Some 39,000 voting cards were distributed at short notice, and the result of the poll was 5,357 in favour of amalgamation with Edinburgh, and 29,891 against. Despite this result, however, the amalgamation went through, with all kinds of angry claims being made, and the plebiscite was regarded as no more than a futile gesture.

The protests which were raised did result in a parliamentary enquiry, but the amalgamation had become inevitable, and there was little choice left in the matter. Perhaps the statement at the enquiry by Gotfried Taylor, a civil engineer, summed up the situation when he said, '*Leith is practically at the end of its life - it cannot grow any more. It has arrived at full age, and there it has got to stop for the rest of its life, unless it extends into Edinburgh, or Edinburgh into Leith, and they become one.*'

Leith Town Council met for the last time on 21 October 1920, under Provost Lindsay, and the robes and insignia of office have not been used since.

A LEITH SAILOR'S TALE

If you have ever had the good fortune to 'splice the mainbrace,' you may have found yourself 'three sheets in the wind,' and knowing that there would probably be 'the devil to pay' when you got home, you have perhaps felt that you had come to the 'bitter end.'

Naughtically (nautically) speaking, to splice the mainbrace means that you have become the victim of excessive drinking, and the term was used during the days of sail when the mainbrace, the strongest sheet, required splicing. This was a difficult job, and in order to compensate the sailors for this task, an extra tot of rum was allowed in addition to their daily ration. A sheet is a rope which is used to turn a sail into position, and if you were to require three sheets, this meant that you had become so unsteady through drink, that even with three sheets to position your sail, you would still not be capable of steering a steady course. The gaps between the planks of a ship's deck were usually plugged by pushing hemp between them, and then caulking with hot tar. This was referred to as 'paying' and as the outermost joint was extremely difficult to do, this became known as the 'devil'. The devil to pay then became the slang for any job or situation which was awkward and difficult to do. If you have come to the bitter end, this means that you have come to the end of the line, and have run out of rope, and this refers to the 'bitt' which is the end of the rope or cable which secures the anchor to any structure.

Having explained your condition to your partner, you would probably have been given a 'clean slate' or an opportunity for a fresh start. This term derives from the days when the progress of the ship was recorded on a slate, and at the end of the watch, this information was entered into the ship's log, and the slate cleaned off, ready for the new watch.

ROAD TO LEITH

To have a face 'as long as Leith Walk' was an expression frequently heard around Leith when reference was being made to someone who seemed a little down in the mouth, but the saying also recognised the importance of the thoroughfare, which is one of the longest in the City.

The original tracks to Leith were by the Quarryholes and by the Calton and these were known as the Easter Road, and the Wester Road. Fate however had a hand to play in the development of the Wester Road, when, in 1650, in order to defend the Town against the Parliamentarians under Oliver Cromwell, General Leslie's army dug a ditch from Holyrood to St. Anthony's Port at the head of the Kirkgate. Alongside this ditch, a huge rampart was built, behind which Leslie's troops lay entrenched. The guns on this high rampart running from Calton Hill to Leith were able to sweep across the flat open ground to the East with their fire. Cromwell's army could not penetrate this defence, and withdrew towards Dunbar. It was the parapet of this great rampart which became the High Walk to Leith, and as it was set some eighteen feet above the adjoining ground level, it became something of a feature, and was described as 'a handsome gravel walk, twenty feet wide, kept in good repair at the public expense.'

In 1722, a company was granted exclusive right to run a coach service along the road, or Low Walk, at the foot of the ramparts, and by 1763, stagecoaches

The Road to Leith : A busy Leith Walk during the dismantling of the iron railway bridge

were running an hourly service. The opening of the North Bridge in 1769 also meant that the road was now the most direct route from the Town to Leith, and traffic and trade began to prosper as a result. The road however, could not withstand the increase in wheeled traffic, and it was in a poor state of repair when, in 1776, the Town let a contract for the reconstruction of the rampart as a single metalled highway. This accounts for the seeming spaciousness of the thoroughfare, and the fact that it is higher than the surrounding levels due to the spreading of huge quantities of the excavated material from the ramparts.

The depression which followed the end of the war with France in 1815 led to high unemployment, and one writer of the day referred to the road to Leith, where passengers in their coaches could witness 'the exhibition of every loathsome object' as they passed by. However, the early 1800s did bring a half-hourly service to Leith, one of which was from the Tron Kirk, and the other from Covenant Close in the High Street. One early feature of the stagecoach service was the stop at Halfway House, where coachmen could rest their horses and carry out any necessary repairs, whilst their passengers could retire to the tavern for a refreshment. A popular drink of the day appears to have been a concoction called 'shrub' which was no doubt consumed in large quantities by the travellers, and this they say gave the name Shrubhill to the location.

Lady Maxwell is recorded as having had a residence at Shrubhill around 1800, and of course the area became one of the City's tramway depots in 1893. Before Shrubhill, the area had a rather more gruesome tale to tell, as it was known as the Gallowlee, a grassy hillock on which the Town's gallows were placed. These were in evidence until the middle of the eighteenth century, but had been removed to become the location of the house called Shrubhill. It is said that much of the soil from the Gallowlee which was excavated at a later date was mixed with the ashes of centuries of wrong-doers who had been hanged on the gibbet, and the mortar was used to build some of the buildings in the New Town.

One famous execution that took place at the Gallowlee was that of the self-confessed murderer John Kelloe, the minister of Spott, near Dunbar, who murdered his wife so that he could marry the daughter of a wealthy laird who was his neighbour.

Many side names still exist down the length of Leith Walk, such as Greenside Place, Cassel's Place and Elm Row, and other names such as Queen's Place, Home's Place and Springfield can still be seen engraved into the stonework of some of the buildings.

A ROYAL VISIT

In 1956, the Queen and the Duke of Edinburgh paid their first royal visit to Edinburgh on board the Royal Yacht Britannia which berthed in the Western Harbour. The Guard of Honour was provided by the 7/9 Battalion the Royal Scots and the bodyguard by Leith High Constables. Eight hundred guests were invited and the sun was reported to have shone all day.

STARRY EYES

Would you believe that Leith once had its own astronomer? He was Mr. Edward Downes, and he was a member of the British Astronomical Association, who spent many hours making observations of the stars from his telescope which he had set on top of a tenement in Henderson Street. The Town Council later gave him permission to establish a small observatory on top of the Giant's Brae where the base can still be seen. Conditions were not too favourable at this location, however, and Mr. Downes began negotiations with the Parks Committee to have his observatory relocated to Victoria Park, and complained about the time being taken by the Council to reach a decision.

TRINITY HOUSE

It is generally accepted that the Institution now known as the Corporation of the Masters and Assistants of the Trinity House of Leith, began in the year 1380. It owed its beginning to the charitable spirit of Leith seafaring men, who imposed a levy called prime gilt on goods loaded or unloaded by Scottish ships in the Port in order to give relief to the poor, aged and infirm in the area. It was from this prime gilt that 'our Lady Kirk of Leith' was founded, and eventually built around the year 1483. The name of the House appears to have varied throughout the years, sometimes referred to as the Fraternity Hospital, the Hospital House of Leith and the Trinity Hospital of Leith, but is now known locally as Trinity House.

The original hospital or almshouse was built in the 16th century, and was located on its present site, and this building survived for some 100 years before an extensive restoration was carried out in 1668. No further alterations were made, but in 1773 a proposal for further works on the building could not be pursued due to the condition of the existing walling, and the possibility of a new building was turned down by a majority vote.

An original proposal to form a large convening room within the existing building was agreed, however, and the work was completed in 1774. The fabric of the old building, which had stood for some 250 years could not be maintained indefinitely, and plans for a new building were prepared by Thomas Brown, Architect, and an estimate of £2,000 for the works was accepted. The foundation stone was laid on June 4th, 1816, and in September 1817 the new Trinity House was ready for occupation. Two inscribed stones are built into the walling of the south gable, one dated 1570, which bears an anchor and two triangles with verses from Psalm 107. The other, dated 1555, refers to the building of the House in the name of The Lord, Masters and Mariners.

This dignified, compact building, in classical style, stands in full view of South Leith Parish Church, and when its doors are open to visitors, it displays many treasures in art and marine history. On the floor of the entrance hall can be seen the crest of the Institution, with its unique coat of arms, and the ancient iron-bound Charter Chest where the documents of the Fraternity were lodged. From the entrance hall, an elegant staircase leads to the Convening Room, and is overlooked by a memorial window which pays tribute to the men of the Merchant Marine who lost their lives during the First World War. The Convening Room at the head of the stairs is entered through mahogany dividing doors, and reveals an ornate plaster ceiling with bold relief work depicting various nautical emblems. The room is dominated by a long mahogany table, and around the walls stand Chippendale ladder-backed chairs, and an armchair made from the remains of a ship on which Hugh Clark, an Edinburgh merchant had spent so many of his years. Around the walls hang portraits by Sir Henry Raeburn, and portraits of many

Trinity House : Sculptured heraldic stones of the Mariners of the Trinity House, Leith, dated 1555

past Masters of the House. There are also several models of ships displayed, and documents and manuscripts of international interest.

Today, Trinity House stands serenely within the Old Kirkgate, reminding us of the days when the Master Mariners of Leith were a substantial influence on the affairs of the Port.

WHALING

The earliest recorded evidence of whaling from Leith dates from 1616, when James VI granted a patent to Sir George Hay and Mr Thomas Murray for whale fishing for a period of thirty-five years, and ten years later Mr Nathaniel Upward was granted a licence to hunt for whales around Greenland. Two ships were fitted out for the purpose with the intention of bringing whale oil into Leith so that it could be used in the manufacture of soap, and a boiling house was later located in the vicinity of Tower Street. The whaling expeditions did not, however, generate an industry until 1750, when the Edinburgh Whale Fishing Company was formed, and the first ship called the *Trial* was specially fitted out, and crewed by men from Leith, Newhaven and Edinburgh. A year later, the *Trial* again sailed to the fishing grounds around Greenland, but this time in company with a new vessel called the *Royal Bounty*, which had the distinction of landing a catch of no fewer than ten whales in Leith in 1754, against the average of five or six.

The early whaling industry did not prove to be profitable : many ships were lost in the ice, and the cost of replacing these became ever more expensive.

Whaling continued from Leith until the early 1840s, however, and at that time the whalers unloaded their cargo of blubber which was taken to The Shore, and then to the boiling-house for making into soap. The partners in the soap company were Christopher and Peter Wood, and their blubber boiling which produced such a noxious smell over Leith was known locally as ' Wood's scent bottle.'

Whaling was revived in Leith when Christian Salvesen & Sons obtained a licence to operate in the Antarctic, and fishing commenced from Leith Harbour in South Georgia in 1909. For the next few years, the whaling industry began to prosper, and the annual sailings from Leith became a great event. Ships became much larger, better processing methods were introduced, and there must have been many young lads from Leith who made the trip South, and earned good money to set them up for their future lives. Whaling of course was not an easy life, and South Georgia was a bleak, inhospitable island, but the demand for whale oil grew, and Salvesen's became the largest whaling business in the world. The oil was used for lamps, lubrication and soap, and in the 1920s it was also used in the making of margarine.

The Second World War took heavy toll of Salvesen's ships and men, but in 1945, the task began to build a modern whaling fleet. Demand began to fall again, and in the early 1950s, the search for whales all but came to an end. Leith Harbour ceased to function in 1961, and whaling ended altogether in 1963.

Despite the conditions and shortages, men still left Leith for South Georgia during the mid fifties, but now travelled first to Glasgow to board the transport vessel *Southern Opal*, which would then call at Tonsberg in Norway, and then Antwerp in Belgium, to pick up personnel. Altogether some 600 men would make their way South, 50% of whom would be British, and the remainder mainly Norwegian.

A great welcome would greet the transport when it arrived at Leith Harbour, as it meant that mail and news from home were delivered to those who had wintered in the harsh Antarctic conditions, spending most of their time repairing the whale catchers in readiness for a new season. Leith Harbour probably produced more barrels of whale oil than Husvik Harbour which was Norwegian-owned, and Grytviken Harbour, which was Argentinian-owned. In a good season some 67,000 barrels were produced, which meant good news for the crews. When the catch was poor, however, a condition referred to as 'whale sickness' would overtake the Harbour, and few smiles would be seen until the season started again. Off periods would be difficult to fill, but there was a local cinema called the 'Kino' which was supplied with up-to-date films and a well stocked library. Christmas and New Year were a particularly difficult time for the men, but there was sure to be a concert arranged, when much hitherto hidden talent was presented, and the usual drag acts gave much laughter.

Conditions were harsh, but there were few vacancies available at signing-on time. Many of those men who had been South but had taken up jobs at home suffered from 'South Georgia sickness,' and the longing to be once again on this bare and barren island.

GI'E THE BA' TAE REILLY

A book about Leith would not be complete without the mention of football and the part played by clubs in the development of the local community. It would also be proper to remind ourselves of a club which bore the Leith name for nearly seventy years, and but for several twists of fortune may have become a force in the Edinburgh football scene. The club was Leith Athletic which was founded in 1887 and which held its first public meetings in the Liberal and Unionist Club near to the Foot of Leith Walk. The club was disbanded in September 1902 but was later reformed and renamed Leith Football Club in 1905. The club was disbanded again in 1916, was reformed in 1919 and renamed Leith Athletic Football Club. The season 1931/32 was a disastrous one for the club, and, despite a brief interlude in the First Division it was not to become a force in Scottish Football. A permanent ground had always been a problem for the club but a new lease was negotiated with the City in 1938 for the use of Meadowbank, providing that ground improvements would be carried out. Leith played their last game against Falkirk Reserves on 27 April 1953 when they lost 2-1. They were eventually expelled from the League in 1954 and wound up in May 1955. The club never managed to recover from it's financial setbacks and the disappointments of the thirties, but there may still be a supporter who will remember the 21,000 crowd that packed into the Marine Gardens in 1931 to see them play Celtic in a relegation battle which they were destined to lose.

Hibernian now carry the Leith banner, and many personal memories are recalled over the past fifty years. Like many other Leith youngsters following football, the yearnings were for the green and white strip. The earliest recollection goes back to 1941 when walking past the foot of Lochend Road with my mother. We could still hear the roar of the crowd from Easter Road, and she stopped to ask a man for the score. '*Eight - wan*' he said as he rushed past, but then he turned, his face wreathed in smiles and shouted '*for Hibs!*'

Names like Sammy Kean, Willie Finnigan, li'le Arthur Milne, Bobby Combe and Gordon Smith were my heroes then, and Rangers players included Jerry Dawson, Tiger Shaw, Willie Woodburn and Alec Venters. How much would they be worth in today's terms one might wonder?

During the war, guest players who had been posted to the Edinburgh area pulled on the green and white strip and these included Matt Busby, Bobby Baxter and Jimmie Caskie, an outside left who later went to Rangers. The late forties and the early fifties were the golden years when Smith, Johnstone, Reilly, Turnbull and Ormond worked their magic over most of the opposition and huge crowds were attracted to the ground. The terracing opposite the main stand was extended to accommodate more fans and a railway halt was built on the Leith Central-Waverley spur. Floodlighting was introduced to the ground and floodlit matches and entry to European competitions made Hibs at that time one of the most progressive of the day and the football world seemed to be at their feet. But what's gone wrong with the game? Fans still go to the matches, they travel to away games, buy season tickets and remain as enthusiastic as ever.

But what's gone wrong with the game? I can still hear the roar of the crowd, remember the names and faces of the stars of the past but its not the same. Its never been the same since that wee man in the crowd at the Dunbar end stopped shouting "*Gi'e the ba' tae Reilly!*".

FIRE ALARMS

There have been several major fires in Leith over the past seventy years, the most recent destroying a former wool store in Great Junction Street. One of the biggest occurred in January 1930 when the grain elevators in Leith Docks caught fire and caused damage estimated at that time to be in the region of £350,000. The fire burned for some thirteen weeks and left local people coughing and spluttering as a result of the pungent fumes. In May 1934, a seed store at McGregor Mills overlooking the Water of Leith was severely damaged and several adjoining properties had to be evacuated.

The Leith Oil and Cake Mills belonging to J&J Cunningham in West Bowling Green Street were extensively damaged by fire in February 1936, and further damaged was caused by a series of explosions. Another major fire in 1936 occurred at the Edinburgh Roperie and Sailcloth's premises in Bath Street where damage was estimated at £425,000. It destroyed the rope walk which was believed to have been the longest of its kind in the country. A smaller fire in 1939 caused damage to the same building after it had been partially rebuilt. One of the most spectacular blazes happened in March 1938 when a timber yard belonging to W&JR Watson in Iona Street was set alight, causing flames to shoot fifty feet into the air and lighting up the night sky over Edinburgh. A children's bonfire which had been burning nearby was said to have been the cause of the outbreak.

A stationery store in Bonnington Road belonging to Andrew Levy was damaged in March 1939 and 400 workers were laid off. In September 1943, A&R Tod's mill premises in North Junction Street were badly damaged by a fire which spread across the road into Prince Regent Street, and in December 1945, premises belonging to George Brown, Ship Repairers, lost tools, machinery and equipment in a blaze at their workshops on The Shore. Around the same time, buildings in Halmyre Street, East Cromwell Street and the Scribbans Kemp biscuit factory in Anderson Place were all badly damaged as a result of fire.

Leith witnessed one of its biggest blazes in June 1955 when premises owned by Hill Thomson in Chapel Lane were destroyed and some 10,000 gallons of rum and whisky were lost, most of it due for overseas markets. In December 1955, tenement properties at 3 Bernard Street and 38 Constitution Street were set alight and 39 residents had to be moved to safety. On a sadder note, three merchant seamen lost their lives in a blaze on board a 6,500 ton ship berthed in the Imperial Dock in May 1956. In March 1961 fire damage was caused to premises owned by Raimes Clark & Co. Ltd, in Smith's Place, and in the late 1970s warehouse premises in Wellington Place were badly damaged and later demolished.

YULETIDE CARDS

In 1841, Charles Drummond, a Leith printer and publisher, produced what is thought to have been the first ever Yuletide card in Britain, and sold it from his shop in the Kirkgate. The idea had come from his friend Thomas Sturrock of Trinity, and the card showed an image of a smiling, chubby-cheeked boy with the greeting: ' A Gude New Year, and mony o' them.'

The first distinctive Christmas Card was produced in London two years later. With the Victorian emphasis on Christmas, it became one of the great annual festivals, and brought a revival of popularity in Edinburgh after its relative obscurity in the years following the Reformation in the sixteenth century.

HAWTHORNS

A very old lady returned to the City in 1957, having spent ninety-six years working in a colliery in Lancashire. She was born in Leith, but her return did not raise much excitement, and she spent some forty years awaiting an opportunity to be rehoused. She was called *Ellesmere*, and was the last surviving working locomotive built by the Leith firm of Hawthorns & Company. Happily, her wait was not in vain, as having been overhauled in the workshops of the Royal Scottish Museum at Granton, she made her last journey to the new extension of the Museum in Chambers Street, where she is now proudly displayed.

In the 1840s, when railways were beginning to expand at home and abroad, locomotive builders were building engines as fast as they could produce them, and it came as no surprise when the firm of R W Hawthorn of Newcastle-on-Tyne acquired the Leith Engineering Works from James B Morton in 1846, in order to set up workshops in Scotland. The first engine built was used by the Edinburgh, Leith and Granton Railway, but a stationary engine worked the incline in the tunnel between Waverley and the former Scotland Street Station until 1868.

In 1857 Hawthorns established Granton Ironworks which had a slipway, but it was not until 1873 that the first ship was built, and engined by the Company. Shipbuilding continued until the 1920s, and a few vessels continued to be built, but mainly from the yard in Leith. One of the last was a yacht for the Archduke of Austria. The works at Granton closed just before the First World War when the Company acquired the firm of S & H Morton. The building and repair of locomotives continued until around 1928 when business came to a standstill, and Hawthorns & Company finally closed.

Ellesmere was named after the Earl of Ellesmere who was at that time Lord Lieutenant of Lancashire. After she arrived home from the South in September 1957, she was housed at Slateford Railway yard. It was hoped that the 19 ton engine could be located in Taylor Gardens, near to the former engineering yard, but the application was turned down by the planners, on the grounds that local amenity would be spoiled !

For the technical, the engine was judged to be unique, being a well tank engine which was designed by Samuel Davison, the Managing Director of Hawthorns.

We will not see *Ellesmere* in Leith again, but she has found a fine resting home, and her plate bearing the names Hawthorns & Co., and Leith will be a reminder of the part played by this local yard during the early days of steam.

MARINE AIRPORT

In 1932 the first passenger carrying service by flying boat was introduced into Scotland, and in July of that year, the *Cloud of Iona* alighted in the Forth off Granton, much to the amazement of those who witnessed it. This flying boat service was being operated from several bases in Scotland by British Flying Boats Ltd., a private company whose Chairman was the Duke of Montrose. It had left the Isle of Wight on the Saturday afternoon after some delays, and the journey was further hampered by strong winds which extended an estimated five or six hour flight by some margin. The boat flew at heights of between five hundred and five thousand feet, was piloted by Lord Malcolm Douglas-Hamilton and Flight Lieutenant Gordon Murray, and took on supplies at Granton before setting off for the Isle of Man.

The aircraft was of the *Saro-Cloud Class* with an all-metal hull, and was driven by two 340 horse power radial air-cooled engines which could carry the craft for some six hours on full fuel. It had seating for ten passengers, and was reported to have been comfortably appointed.

Eighteen years later, Lord Provost Sir Andrew Murray welcomed the first aircraft of Aquila Airways to touch down at Leith Marine Airport on the opening of a new service from Southampton to Edinburgh, and then Greenock and back. This aircraft was a *Hythe Class* flying boat, and was on a proving flight with the intention of commencing a regular weekly service scheduled to begin on 7 July 1950, with a further service due to operate between Southampton and Glasgow.

BOAC had been flying their *Solent Class* flying boats on their South African services, but when these were withdrawn, Aquila Airways became the only commercial operator using flying boats in the country, and these were believed to have been the first services of this kind to have been introduced into Britain. For their part, the Dock Commission was to supply and maintain the necessary mooring buoys, would also arrange for suitable firefighting facilities to be made available, and would provide a tender to convey passengers ashore. The Ministry of Civil Aviation also required that a controlled landing area at least 6,000 feet in length should be available in two directions, and wind directors were also to be provided. Aquila Airways had projected that a fare of £9 single and £16 4/-return would apply for journeys from Southampton, which compared favourably with rail fares at that time, and had the added attraction of having a flight time of only two hours.

Leith Marine Airport : A Sunderland flying boat moored off the Albert Dock after its inaugural flight from Southhampton

On June 2, the inaugural flight took off from Southampton, following a route over Bristol, Worcester and the Lake District, flying at a speed of around 160 mph. It touched down in Leith where it moored off the Albert Dock. A launch conveyed the passengers ashore where it was met by a reception party, including Lord Provost Sir Andrew Murray, James Hoy, MP for Leith, Mr George Veitch, Chairman of Leith Dock Commission, and representatives of the Navy and Air Force. The service was officially declared open, and after the reception, the flying boat left Leith for Greenock, and then continued its return journey to Southampton, having covered an 800 mile round trip.

Four weeks after the opening of this new service, Aquila Airways indicated that it would have to be postponed due to lack of interest, and prospects for a resumption were not encouraging, due to increases in fuel costs, and more stringent requirements made by the Civil Aviation authority. The Dock Commission continued to renew the annual licence, but the only users of the facilities were several American *Mariner* flying boats which landed there in 1952. The airport licence was held until 1959, when no civil flying boat operators were then in business, and the Dock Commissioners finally withdrew their application.

'THE NAVY'S HERE'

The first few months of the Second World War had not gone well for the Royal Navy, with the sinking of many ships, but on 17 December 1939, came better news, which was the scuttling of the German pocket battleship *Graf Spee* at the mouth of the River Plate. This action by *Ajax*, *Achilles* and *Exeter* was the basis for the classic war film *The Battle of the River Plate*, but the story as far as Leith was concerned was only beginning.

Far from the scene of this action, the *Graf Spee's* supply ship *Altmark* had been keeping out of reach in the South Atlantic, and her Captain Dau decided to make a run for home via Greenland, Iceland and the coast of Norway. On board *Altmark* were 299 British seamen who had been taken prisoner from ships sunk by the *Graf Spee* in the Atlantic, and Captain Dau must have been beginning to raise his hopes of reaching his home port in Germany, when his ship was spotted by Hudson aircraft, and a confirmed sighting was made of *Altmark* near Bergen. Destroyers from the Fourth Flotilla based at Rosyth tried to make *Altmark* heave to for boarding, but she sought the refuge of Norwegian territorial waters.

An attempt was made to enter the fiord by *HMS Cossack*, commanded by Captain Vian, but he was informed that the *Altmark* had already been searched but no prisoners were found. Norway was neutral at the time and the situation was causing a problem for the Admiralty. The Commander of Fourth Flotilla, Captain Vian, in *HMS Cossack*, attempted to enter the fjord, but was approached by one of the Norwegian gun boats, and was assured that *Altmark* had already been searched. *HMS Cossack* entered Jossing Fiord and boarded a Norwegian gun boat, but negotiations to free the prisoners were not successful. After an unsuccessful attempt to escape from the fiord, *Altmark* attempted to ram *HMS Cossack* but only succeeded in running aground. The boarding party jumped onto the deck of the *Altmark* and with the crew still trying to free the ship, shots were exchanged. The boarding party made their way below deck and in response to the shouts of British seamen, the answer came, 'Well the Navy's here! Come on out of it.' Rumours of something big about to happen spread through Leith, and within a few hours *HMS Cossack* docked to a tremendous welcome and the 299 seamen were grateful to be on home soil again.

A FATAL DUEL

Three days before Christmas 1789, the lonely wasteground where Seafield Baths once stood was the scene of a fatal duel between Mr. Francis Foulke of Dublin and an army officer whose name was not disclosed. The Edinburgh Magazine of that year merely states that they had quarrelled, and posted each other at a coffee house, which was the fashion of the day. A challenge took place, and they met, each attended by a second. They fired their pistols twice without effect, but so bitter was their dispute that they reloaded, fired a third time, and Foulke fell with a ball to his heart.

Foulke was a medical student at the university where he had shown considerable talent, and in the previous year he had been elected President of the Natural History Society, and of the Royal Medical Society of Edinburgh.

ST ANTHONY'S PRECEPTORY

The remains of St Anthony's Monastery were finally demolished during the latter half of the nineteenth century where it had stood on the West side of St Anthony's Lane at the Henderson Street end. It had been erected there by

Sir Robert Logan of Restalrig in 1430, and was dedicated to religious uses by Henry Wardlaw, the Bishop of St Andrews, and was the only house of its kind belonging to that Order in Scotland.

St Anthony was the patron saint and protector of the lower animals, especially swine, and he is usually represented as having a pig for a page, probably on account of his having lived on roots, in common with the hogs of the desert. On the common seal of the Leith Monastery, he is represented under a canopy, wearing a hermit's gown, and having a wild pig with a bell on its neck beside his right foot.

The Seal of the Preceptory of St Anthony

He is said to have lived in an old castle overlooking the Nile, and after his death the body was hidden by two of his disciples until some two hundred years later when it was discovered and taken to Alexandria where it was laid to rest in the church of St John the Baptist. After a lapse of a further seventy years, the remains are said to have been taken to Constantinople, and then to Vienne in France in 1089 where, under the influence of the saintly dust, miracle cures were reported.

There was an outbreak of erysipelas in Europe around this period which proved to be prevalent in the Dauphiny region, and the prayers which were offered at the shrine of St Anthony are said to have cured the outbreak. The disease became known as St Anthony's Fire, and it is perhaps the reason why Sir Robert Logan chose this particular Order to come to Leith, as he himself may have suffered from this same disease, and benefited from the spiritual learnings of the Order.

St Anthony's was a small, poor foundation with only a few canons in residence at any one time, and the area known as Yardheads closely followed the boundary of the Preceptory. The canons' income came from wine, and for every tun landed at Leith, one quart went to St Anthony's, and occasionally the wine was auctioned to the wine merchants of Edinburgh. The canons were very much involved with the community, and used the income from their wine sales to relieve some of the hardships found in the town, and provided some comfort for the sick and aged. The small chapel within the Preceptory was also used to train local boys to read and sing, and the local incorporations also worshipped there until the accommodation became too small.

The Preceptory was partially destroyed during the Siege of Leith, and in 1596 the entire lands and revenues were made over to the Kirk Session of South Leith Church, which were used to build King James VI Hospital within the south west corner of the churchyard. The Kirk Session also elected an official called the

Baron Baillie of St Anthony, and he exercised considerable jurisdiction in Leith and Newhaven until this office was discontinued in 1833. The last Baron Baillie was Thomas Barker, a relative of Dr Robertson, the author of '*The Sculptured Stones of Leith*'.

Tradition has it that St Anthony's Chapel, which stands in ruins on Arthur's Seat above St Margaret's Loch, had close links with St Anthony's Preceptory in Leith, and it is said to have guarded a sacred fountain which was once known for the healing power of its waters. Others have suggested that the Chapel was a kind of ecclesiastical custom house which could provide a look-out point for ships in the Forth from which revenue could be extracted for the benefit of the Abbey of Holyrood. It has also been suggested that a light hanging in the tower could have attracted the attention of seamen sailing in the Forth who, in cases of danger, might have been inclined to make vows to this particular saint.

MORTONS PATENT SLIP

The Morton family business was started before 1773 by Hugh Morton, who was a wright in the Kirkgate. The business passed to his son Samuel, a cartwright, around 1807, and Samuel's son Hugh joined the business in 1834. The firm then absorbed the shipbuilding business of Thomas Morton, who was another son of Hugh Morton, and a brother of Samuel.

In 1819 Thomas Morton invented his patent slip, which was a method of dragging ships out of the water onto dry land, where necessary repairs and overhauls could be undertaken. The Leith Register of 1864 made the following report: '*while wooden shipbuilding has been delaying, iron ships and steam packet building with engines and boiler making has been established by the well known firm of Hugh Morton & Co., who also erected the first patent slip here. The business is still carried on with that energy which deserves the success it has attained as evinced by the crowded throng of skilled workmen employed by the firm, both at their large establishments at the Wet Docks and their other one in Leith Walk*.'

Morton's patent slip had many advantages over a dry dock. For instance it cost less, and could be built within a confined space. It also gave good access to the hull of the vessel for carrying out repairs, and working conditions generally were much better. At one time, the slip was being used by many of the large dockyards in the UK and overseas.

Thomas Morton, who patented the slip, died in 1832, and the ownership of the patent passed into the hands of Hugh and Samuel who, from 1834 onwards, styled themselves as 'patent slip makers.' The firm of S & H Morton was engaged in many engineering activities, and from 1834 until 1900 was listed as makers of agricultural implements, patent slip builders, iron ship builders, engineers and boiler makers. Indeed, several of the steamships built by the firm were also engined by them.

The firm continued after the death of Hugh in 1878, until 1910, when it was taken over by R W Hawthorn of Newcastle, which in 1846 had acquired the Leith Engine Works at Sheriff Brae from James B Maxton & Co.

It is said that Morton Street, now Academy Street, had been named after Hugh Morton, where he lived during his later years, and the Thomas Morton Hall in Ferry Road is named after the inventor of the patent slip which was such an innovation in its day.

MELROSE'S TEA

Andrew Melrose, whose name bore the famous firm of tea makers in Leith, died in 1855. The East India Company had held the monopoly of tea dealing for several years, but in 1833, this monopoly was abolished, and this presented opportunities for trade with China and India. Andrew Melrose had set up shop in the Canongate with his partners, and with others, he organised the first shipment of tea into Leith when the chartered vessel *Isabella* returned in 1835. Andrew's son William joined his father in the business, and for a time, Melroses was one of the principal stores in Princes Street.

THIN RED LINE

Many people may have wondered where that boundary line between Edinburgh and Leith ran - the thin red dividing line which had caused much friction, and not a little humour over a period of many years. On the East side, it came from a point between the Eastern General Hospital and Craigentinny Golf Course, and followed a line sighted on the spire of the Tron Church to Lochend Loch, where it then ran West to Pilrig, down the centre line of Pilrig Street and Newhaven Road, to the junction with Ferry Road, and then turned along the centre line of Ferry Road to Granton Road, where it ran through the rear gardens of the villas on the West side, and continued a line through the former Queensberry Lodge, Wardie Square and Lower Granton Road to finish just to the East of the breakwater. Hibs football ground at Easter Road just made it into the old Leith boundary, but the nearby Norton Park School, although an Edinburgh school was almost entirely within the Leith limit. The line ran just to the South of the Eastern Cemetery, and after crossing Easter Road it followed a diagonal line through the

© Walter Taylor

The Thin Red Line : A small boy stretches his legs between Edinburgh and Leith

tenement properties in Albert Street, and then Buchanan Street, to cut through into Leith Walk at what is now the City Limits Bar. Prior to the amalgamation, the bar was run by James Munro, Wine and Spirit Merchant, and it is said that because of the difference in licensing hours you could drink in the Leith side of the bar until closing time, and then move further up the bar and cross the boundary line, which meant that you could have another half-hour's drinking under the Edinburgh licensing hours.

The boundary line between Leith and Edinburgh also passed through many of the tenement properties in Albert Street and Buchanan Street, and at that time when these flats consisted of a room, kitchen, W.C. and coal cellar, it was theoretically possible to have your meal in the kitchen on the Leith side and go to bed in Edinburgh at night.

SURE AND STEDFAST

Perhaps no other youth organisation in Leith has had a greater effect on the community than the Boys' Brigade, and few have not at some time, witnessed their displays, shows and pantomimes, held in churches and local halls. It seems as if everyone has had a relative or friend who was a member of the Boys' Brigade, and the Battalion was proud that until recently it had remained as a local organisation.

In 1883, William Smith founded his Boys' Brigade in Glasgow, and some four years later, the organisation arrived in Leith, when three Companies were formed by Mr J Scott Wight. A further Company was started by Mr L MacFadyen in what was then known as the Stanwell Hall in Bonnington Road. Unfortunately, these did not survive, but a group of churchmen did succeed in forming a sufficient number of Companies to qualify as a Battalion, and on 5th October 1900, the Leith Battalion was officially enrolled at Brigade Headquarters. Since then, the Battalion has played a prominent part in many local and national events, and celebrated its own 25th, 50th and 75th anniversaries with a series of special events.

To mark the Centenary of the founding of the Boys' Brigade in 1883, a May Fair was held in Lethem Park, where various events and exhibitions took place, the proceeds from which were donated to local charities, and the section of the Walkway known as Stedfastgate was also formed as part of these Centenary celebrations.

Mr Alexander John Lethem was one of the leading figures in the Boys' Brigade movement, and he identified himself particularly with the Leith Battalion. He was responsible for the founding of the Boys' Brigade Memorial Club in Ferry Road, but perhaps his greatest gift was the acquisition of the recreational park now known as Lethem Park. The park was significantly enhanced in 1958 when, through the generosity of Sir John Pollock, Bart., adjoining property was purchased and developed as the Pollock Pavilion, with canteen, changing facilities and committee rooms.

A J Lethem also started camps at Cloan near Auchterarder, and at Upper Cloan Farm, and a cairn bearing inscriptions was erected in 1940 by senior members and ex-members of the 1st Leith Battalion.

In September 1998, The Leith Battalion was dissolved and a new 'Edinburgh, Leith and District Battalion' was formed.

It was William A Smith, founder of the Boys' Brigade who said that "*it is no accident that The Boys' Brigade spells Boy with a capital B. The old order when boys were to be seen and not heard has passed. Today, his is the most claimant voice in the world. He cannot be ignored. The world cannot do without him. He is the hope for the future, the hope of the race; certainly he is the hope of The Church.*"

THE PIPES

One day in the middle of 1934, an old well was discovered underneath a pavement in Lochend Road, and beside it were two wooden pipes which were believed to have once carried a water supply for industrial use from Lochend Loch to Leith during the early years of the nineteenth century. The pipes were likened to young trees which had been stripped of their bark, bored through the centre and laid end to end. Despite the fact that they had remained in their original position for nearly a century, they were reported to have been in good condition. The old well which had been uncovered was around seventeen feet deep, and was infilled and made good with material from the site which was being excavated.

The lack of a good supply of water had been a problem for the inhabitants of Leith, as during the early years this was provided by the Water of Leith, the Greenside Burn and the Broughton Burn, but these sources were polluted, and the public wells which were available were few and far between. Industry too in Leith could not expand due to the lack of a piped water supply, but a plan was produced, and a scheme to use Lochend Loch as the reservoir was promoted. However, it was not long before it became clear that the supply from the loch would fall far short of requirements, and the scheme was abandoned in favour of a piped supply from a large cistern located at the junction of Water Street and Tolbooth Wynd and known locally as 'the pipes.'

CHAIN PIER

The Chain Pier comprised three spans suspended from iron chains, and ran out to sea for a length of 500 feet from its location opposite Trinity Crescent. It was constructed by Captain Brown of the Royal Navy, and was opened in 1821, having cost £4,000 to build. It was four feet wide, and had a depth at low water of from five to six feet, and it served steam packets to Stirling, Queensferry and other ports in the Forth. Improvements to Leith Docks, and the opening of Granton Harbour in 1833 saw its use decline, and it was used mainly by bathers, and was once the headquarters of the Forth Swimming Club. In 1840, it became the property of the Alloa Steam Packet Company, but by 1852 it was already decaying, and it was eventually dismantled around the turn of the century. The former booking office is now the Chain Pier bar.

DARIEN SCHEME AND THE WORCESTER

Not only did Dumfries-born William Paterson found the Bank of England, but he became the driving force behind what was to become known as the Darien Scheme, the first expedition of which left Leith in July 1698. Twelve hundred colonists sailed to Central America in the hope that they could challenge the trading influences of the East India Company in order that Scotland could once again regain her traditional importance. Not much more than a year later, however, the expedition was forced to return with more than half the number dead through fever, and with Fort St Andrew in Caledonia Bay abandoned. English settlers in Jamaica had refused to assist the plight of the Scots, and this only served to increase the friction which was affecting Anglo-Scottish relations.

Later, a ship called the *Annandale*, belonging to the Darien Company was seized in the Thames and sold, and an English East Indiaman called the *Worcester* put into Burntisland in order to have some repairs carried out. Some members of the crew unfortunately began to boast that they had captured a Darien ship in Eastern waters, and had murdered her captain and crew. This story was reinforced by the fact that a Scottish ship called the *Speedy Return* had not been heard of, and the rumours of her fate were similar to those described by the crew of the *Worcester*. The captain and crew were arrested, and despite the lack of evidence, the sentence of death was passed on all. There was some unease at the decision, however, and some felt that it would simply inflame future relationships with the English, but the cry for vengeance grew stronger, and on the appointed day of the execution, a large section of the population gathered at the Cross, and in Parliament Square. Scuffles broke out when the crowd believed that the crew were going to be reprieved, and it became clear that the only way that the crowd would be appeased was for the Council to yield to the execution of some members of the crew.

Thousands gathered in Leith to witness the hanging of Captain Green, the first mate Madder, and Simpson the gunner. They went on foot through the Canongate, escorted by the Town Guard to a point where a battalion of the Foot Guards and a body of the Horse Guards were drawn up, and the three were hanged upon a gibbet erected within high water mark on the sands of Leith. The three men denied their guilt until the last, and it is said that Captain Drummond of the *Speedy Return* was believed to have been found later, fit and well in India.

LEITH SAILORS' HOME

The first Sailors' Home in Leith was opened in 1840 in premises which still exist in Dock Place, but in 1853 a new Home was founded by Admiral William Hall, who had close family links with Leith. The Home, which was completed in the mid 1880s, stands on The Shore, and was designed in Baronial style by CCS Johnston, and built at a cost of some £10,000. The original Home in Dock Place was converted into the Mercantile Marine Department and Government Navigation School in 1882.

Leith Sailors Home before refurbishment

The new Home could accommodate 56 seamen and 9 officers, and the facilities included a restaurant, clothing store, reading room, and dining and recreation rooms, which could be converted to accommodate lectures or concerts. Lord Rosebery journeyed over 400 miles to open the Home before a large and fashionable crowd, and declared that "*this Home is the island of Great Britain on which we stand at this moment.*"

After the Second World War, the need for a Home of this type gradually diminished, and for a few years the building was known locally as the Angel Hotel. The property stood empty for several years until it was refurbished in 1994.

ZEPPELIN RAID

During the night of April 2nd 1916, a Zeppelin raid took place on Leith and Edinburgh which resulted in loss of life and damage to property. The Zeppelin appeared over Leith around midnight, and taking Leith Docks and the Water of Leith as its guide, the airship followed a circular course, and dropped several bombs and incendiaries as it passed overhead. The first fell on the docks itself, damaging two small craft, and severely damaging a large bonded store nearby. Bombs also fell along The Shore causing minor damage, but an elderly man was killed at home in Commercial Street, and the manse of St. Thomas' Church in Mill Lane was damaged. Damage to property was also reported in Anderson Place, and a small child was killed. Nine high explosive and twelve incendiary bombs were dropped on Leith during this raid.

DRINK AND BE THANKFUL

This is not a phrase which would be supported by Alcoholics Anonymous, but it does give a clue to the connection between an Edinburgh lady called Catherine Sinclair, a disappearing fountain and The Leith Battalion, The Boys' Brigade.

Catherine was born in 1800, the fourth daughter of Sir John and Lady Diana Sinclair, and she became one of the most respected ladies of her era through her writings, concerns for the poor, and the opening of 'cooking depots' to provide meals at low cost for those in need. However, it was her provision of a drinking fountain which was to lead to much newspaper comment over a period of years, and end at Stedfastgate at the Leith end of the Walkway at Gosford Place.

The drinking fountain, which was the first to be erected in Edinburgh was placed at the junction of Lothian Road and Princes Street in 1859, but some fourteen years later, the City fathers required its removal due to the increase in traffic volume. Such was the reaction to this announcement, and to the respect which many had for the work done by Catherine Sinclair, that the plan to remove the fountain was withdrawn. It remained in position until 1932, when City officials, this time moving with unusual haste, removed it to one of the Burgh Engineer's yards in the Cowgate before much public opposition could be raised. It had been thought that the fountain would be re-erected in some other location, but in 1934 it still lay in the Burgh Engineer's yard.

The Fountain : An image of the Sinclair Fountain as it might have been in 1859

The matter was raised through the newspaper columns at regular intervals, and was still believed to be in the Burgh Engineer's Yard in 1964, but a later investigation into the fate of the fountain made by the Evening News led them to an overgrown yard in Bonnington Road, where they discovered the stone remains of the Sinclair Fountain, which was confirmed after clearing away much of the debris, and uncovering the stone with the inscription reading 'Drink and be Thankful.'

It was not considered possible to rebuild the fountain, but a happy ending was in sight. To mark the Centenary of The Boys' Brigade in 1983, the Leith

Battalion launched a Walkway Appeal, and funds were raised to plant trees and landscape a section of the new walkway along the former railway cutting to Victoria Park, now named Stedfastgate. Beside the plaque commemorating the opening by Lord Provost Tom Morgan has been erected the last remaining stones of the Sinclair Fountain, which recognises the wonderful work done by an Edinburgh lady who gave her life to easing some of the pain of poverty during the 1800s.

THE GREETIN' MEETING

On a cold November evening in 1920, one of the most significant moments in Leith's long past was held in the Council Chamber, when Provost Lindsay, and his colleagues and guests marked the end of the Town Council, and of the Burgh as a separate entity. The Provost received his guests in his room beforehand, and when all had gathered, they adjourned to the Council Chamber where the tables had been prepared for a meal.

The Provost occupied his usual chair at the head of the Chamber, and on his right were seated Lord Salvesen, Sir Malcolm Smith, Colonel James Mackay, Bailie Finlayson, Mr James Currie, the Rev William Swan and Mr Robert Cross. On the left were seated Sir Richard Mackie, Mr J W Hope, Mr Theodore Salvesen, Bailie Muirhead, Mr William Thomson, Mr James Roger and Mr Robert Smith. Many Leith businesses were also represented including M P Galloway, A & R Tod, Menzies & Co, George Gibson & Co, Bruce Lindsay Brothers, Cran & Somerville, George Gibson & Co., and Councillors, Council Officers and officials also attended.

The meal by all accounts was exceptional, and after all had settled down and the toast to the King honoured, Mr James Currie rose to give 'The Port of Leith'

The Greetin' Meeting : The last Town Council meeting before Leith lost its independence in 1920

He said that it was perhaps natural that someone who had been closely involved with mercantile shipping should have a balanced outlook on matters, but he had been bound to say that he had seen nothing which had made him change his view that the amalgamation with Edinburgh could be looked upon as a very distinct public loss. Leith had a long and chequered history he said, and there was no doubt that in prehistoric times, the estuary of the Water of Leith must have become a refuge for their primitive ancestors. To a background of some laughter, he continued by saying that with such a history behind them, there was little doubt that they should also be able to survive the embraces of Edinburgh. He looked forward to the continuing development and prosperity of the area, and proposed the toast of The Port of Leith, coupled with the name of Sir Richard Mackie.

Sir Richard, in reply, said that he had lived in Leith since 1865, had seen many changes take place during that time, and reminded the guests that vessels of any size had once to unload at Granton. The Town Council had ceased at midnight on Monday he continued, and amid some laughter, he said that the Provost's chain could now go back to its donor, for he had already made a claim for its return. He was pleased that the Port of Leith was to retain its name, and hoped that everyone would continue to do everything possible to advance the interests of the town.

Lord Salvesen, in proposing the toast of 'The Corporation of Leith', said that the gathering was a unique occasion for himself, and recalled that his earliest connection with Leith dated from 1857. He had now achieved one of his fondest ambitions, and that was to be sitting as a guest of the Provost of Leith within the walls of the Chamber, and he reminded guests that never again would a gathering of this kind take place. He continued to say that there could be no higher tribute to the Corporation and its activities in the interests of the community, than the plebiscite which had twice recorded the opinion of the citizens. They had fought the battle courageously, and he was convinced that the community had approved of the action that had been taken, and he now had pleasure in proposing the toast to the Corporation.

Bailie Finlayson, in reply, thanked Lord Salvesen for his kind words, and said that the Corporation had endeavoured to promote the interests of the community, and could think of no better contribution than the £20,000 which had been donated by Mr Hope towards the Leith Memorial Fund. In his reply, Mr Hope said that it had been over forty years since he had been in Leith, having served his apprenticeship in the town, and his contribution towards the Memorial Fund was only a small repayment towards the memory of some of the friendships that he had made there.

The Provost proposed the health of his colleagues, and said that the dinner marked the end of his three-year term of office, and of the end of the Town Council of Leith, but he hoped that those who were candidates for the greater Corporation would maintain a practical interest in the Port. Sir Malcolm Smith proposed the health of Provost Lindsay, and the dinner ended with the singing of 'For he's a jolly good fellow.' Finally, the Provost's Chain of Office was presented to Trinity House, and the Mace to the Dock Commission, these having previously been donated to the Council by Sir Richard Mackie and Sir Malcolm Smith.

So ended one of the most important periods in Leith's long history, and the commencement of the amalgamation with Edinburgh.

CHANGING TIMES

The years after the Second World War saw Leith facing yet another one of those crises which has dogged the port over many centuries. Shipping practices began to change, and the trade in basic commodities began to achieve a new importance. The Dock Commissioners had never been slow to appreciate the changing situation, and in 1944 a new and wider entrance to the Port was obtained as a result of the construction of the East and West breakwaters. 1953 saw the completion of two new deep-water berths in the Western Harbour, and the industrial development of land within the dock estate. However, the need for deep water was crucial to the future development of Leith as a port, and a scheme for a new entrance lock and sealing dam was commissioned, and commenced in 1965, in order to create a non-tidal impounded harbour, and a new entrance to the existing Imperial Dock.

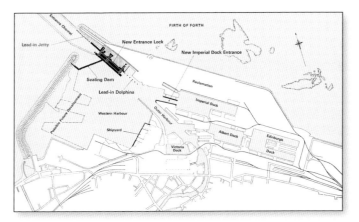

Leith Entrance Lock : The plan for the provision of deep water facilities by means of an entrance lock

This scheme enabled ships drawing 35 feet to enter the port, which was sufficient for the standard bulk carrier at that time. Deep water was also provided at all existing berths, and in addition, the future development of Western Harbour was made more economical by reducing quay wall heights by 17 feet, thus reducing difficult dredging operations. The impounding of the docks included the construction of a 2,100 foot long coffer dam enclosing the lock area, together with a sealing dam which cut off the length from the West Breakwater to the new Entrance Lock. The Entrance Lock itself is some 1,000 feet long, and 110 feet wide, with gates at each end forming a main chamber 850 feet long, which can be divided into smaller chambers if necessary. The lock gates are of the caisson type, and are retracted into chambers on the East wall.

It was estimated that the total amount of concrete required for the lock was 235,000 cubic yards, which was batched over a period of 16 months at the rate of 5,000 cubic yards per week, the batching plant itself being located on site. A concrete lead-in jetty was also constructed as an extension to the East wall, and the approach channel was realigned and deepened over a distance of some threequarters of a mile.

The work commenced in May 1965, and was officially opened by the Duke of Edinburgh in May 1969. The Dock Commissioners were no longer in existence at this time, as on 1 January 1968 the Forth Ports Authority began to administer all of the ports around the river as a single unit, and in 1992 the docks became part of Forth Ports plc.

Today, the work of the docks goes on, but to the onlooker it is the sight of cruise liners from all parts of the world berthed in the Western Harbour which holds the attention, and perhaps should remind us that the development which we see around us today might not have been possible had it not been for the vision of the Dock Commissioners, when they decided over thirty years ago that the future of the port lay in the provision of deep water facilities.

FIFIES, SCAFFIES, ZULUS AND BALDIES

If you ever happen to visit the British Science Museum in London, you may see a fine model of a Leith Baldie which was a fishing boat which began to be seen in the Firth of Forth around the 1870s.

The Fifie was built to no set design, but all had the same characteristics of vertical stern, deep heel and forefront, and hollow, rising floors. The larger boats were carvel built, and were rigged with a large, dipping lug sail, and a standing lug mizzen. They ranged from 36 to 60 feet in length overall.

Scaffies were a variation of the Fifie, as was the Zulu, which was built and named after the Zulu War in 1879. The Leith Baldie was again a smaller variation of the Fifie, and was carvel built and decked, and used for small line fishing. They would vary from 24 to 30 feet in length.

It was not until 1882 that trawling was introduced into Aberdeen, and Leith and Granton soon followed as trawling ports, but line fishing and drifting still continued. A typical wooden trawler was the *Hawk*, which was built at Leith in 1882. It was 87 feet long, with a beam of 18 feet, and was carvel built and schooner rigged. A two stage expansion engine supplied steam at 85 pounds pressure, which powered a single three blade propeller.

KELLY GANG

The evening of February 4th 1881 proved to be quite an eventful one, with shootings and robberies reported from several parts of Edinburgh, resulting in the police force being placed on full alert.

In Leith that evening Sergeants Arnott and Reid from the Leith Force carried out their usual patrol around the Custom House, and returning there some time later, observed two men peering into a window at the rear of the building. The officers confronted the men who, at first could give no satisfactory account of themselves, but then said that they belonged to a ship berthed in the docks, but as the policemen knew that such a vessel did not exist, they were asked to accompany the two Sergeants to the Police Station. As the group turned the corner at Dock Place, Sergeant Arnott was shot in the head, but despite his wounds he managed to blow his whistle for assistance. Sergeant Reid, who had started to pursue the men into Commercial Street was also shot, but fortunately Constable John Cameron, who had been on duty nearby had been alerted by the sounds of the whistle, and despite being threatened with a revolver, started to pursue the two men along Commercial Street in the direction of Newhaven, each running on opposite sides of the road. At the railway gate leading to the Commercial Dock , Constable Alexander Nicholson, having heard the police whistles, attempted to intercept the men, one of whom fired a shot at him, injuring him in the leg, but despite this he continued in pursuit. Three other Constables in the area gave chase, and further shots were fired, one narrowly missing Constable McConville, who confronted one of the men called Seymour at the dock wall, but before he could be arrested he put his gun to his mouth, and killed himself.

Meanwhile, Constable Nicholson continued his pursuit of the man called Grant, who was becoming exhausted, and whose revolver appeared to have jammed, but the chase continued into Albany Street, then into Argyle Street, and finally into Hope Street, where he was confronted by Constable Nicholson. Grant attempted to take his own life by aiming the revolver at his head, but the trigger had well and truly jammed. The Constables, now with their prisoner, retraced their steps to Commercial Street at the foot of Admiralty Street, where Constable McConville was guarding the body of Seymour surrounded by a small group of people. Seeing his companion lying dead, Grant was heard to say, 'I wish I was beside him.' The body was removed to Leith Hospital, and Grant was escorted to the Police Station by a strong body of policemen.

On the Saturday afternoon, a large crowd gathered in front of the Police Station, where the Superintendent of Police directed the Court Officer to bring in James Grant, who was described as a labourer, residing in Edinburgh. He was charged with having discharged firearms with intent to murder, and having, in conjunction with Thomas Seymour, now deceased, had wilfully, maliciously and unlawfully fired shots from a revolver at Sergeants Reid and Arnott and Constable Nicholson, to the danger of their lives. Grant listened with some indifference to the charges, and was sent for trial at Edinburgh High Court on May 24 1881, where he was sentenced to fourteen years penal servitude.

There was a belief in some quarters that the two men in this affair had been part of the Ned Kelly Gang from Australia, and had recently arrived by ship from Melbourne, but it is more likely that they were simply two armed thugs with assumed names, who had failed to get the better of a vigilant Leith Police Force.

CENTRAL KINEMA

Picture theatres were at the height of their popularity after the end of the First World War, and local picture houses were attracting capacity audiences at every showing. At that time, Leith had a population of between 80,000 and 90,000, and with the continuing growth of the cinema, accommodation was not keeping up with demand.

It was as a result of this demand, that the Central Cinema Company planned to erect and operate a cinema in Hope Street, now Casselbank Street, near to the Foot of Leith Walk. The premises had been used previously as a turkish baths, and Mr J W Hodgson, the proprietor of the baths became managing director of the new company. Under his own supervision, and from the plans which had been prepared by the Architect, Mr George Craig, the former baths were transformed into one of the finest picture houses around at that time. Comfort and elegance had been the priorities for the building, and with fine attractions to call upon, it was hoped that this new venture would attract a good following.

The external walls of the existing building were raised by some thirteen feet, and the new flat roof was of concrete, supported by steel beams. Internally, nothing remained of the once well-appointed turkish baths and the dwelling house to the front, and in their place a fine hall was constructed and tastefully decorated. The picture house was capable of seating some four hundred persons on the main ground floor, with a further hundred seated in a small balcony area. The large proscenium gave good space for the picture, and a special feature was a fine coloured representation of the Leith coat of arms. An orchestra pit had been formed so that spectators could have an unobstructed view of the performance. A high pressure heating system was installed, ventilation ensured a clean flow of air at all times, and the projection room was suitably fireproofed and equipped with two projectors, which were the most up to date available at that time. The tip-up seats were upholstered in old gold, and were reported to have been very comfortable

The picture house was opened in November 1920, and was widely acclaimed for its varied programme, and accomplished orchestra. Prices ranged from ninepence and one shilling for the stalls, to one and sixpence for the balcony, and there was a continuous programme from 3pm until 10.30pm, six days a week. Early screenings included *False Gods* and *Man of Honour*, accompanied by an interest film, comedy and Pathe Gazette all on one show. The picture house appears to have closed sometime during the early 1930s, and has since been used as a Pentecostal Church, but it is probably still one of the best-preserved cinemas in Edinburgh.

AN EVIL OMEN

On the 28th and 29th March 1625 the East coast of Scotland was affected by a great storm. The water in the harbour at Leith rose to a height never known before, causing great damage to ships and some deaths by drowning. This phenomenon was regarded by the superstitious as a sign that some dreadful happening had taken place, and sure enough, it was confirmed that King James VI had died the day before, on 27th March.

'DOON THE CHANNEL'

One of the places which we hear so many Leith people still speaking about is the 'old Kirkgate', and the redevelopment of this area which effectively clawed the very heart out of the community.

What was it like during its heyday you may ask? Well, a typical Saturday night would mean that the week's work was done, and people would crowd 'doon the Channel' to do their shopping. Street sellers would be out in force along Junction Road or Great Junction Street as we now know it, and at the Foot of the Walk, free-speechers would be on their soap boxes telling listeners how to sort out all the ills of the world. Some sellers would also be at their stalls trying to tempt you with all the bargains of the day, and their repartee would be the cause of much laughter by the passing crowds. Many folk would have come to do their shopping, but others would go to meet up with their friends, because the Kirkgate was the social centre of Leith around which the universe revolved.

'Doon the Channel' : The Final Days of the Kirkgate before demolition and the redevelopment of the area during the sixties

111

Everyone seemed to know each other, and the air would be full of the sound of conversation which would give it a real buzz. You might stop at Scott the Hatter, or the Ting Tong Tea Company, or Guthrie's the butcher where you could buy a steaming hot pig's foot which you might eat as you continued your shopping. Jock Ward's chip shop was renowned for the chips, but you could also buy beetroot, and just a few doors away 'Big Albert', who was Italian, sold fish suppers, and often listened to records of Caruso which he played on a small phonograph with a large sound horn. One day it was said that someone poured some of Albert's hot peas and vinegar down the horn, and to the amusement of his customers in the shop he roared, 'who chuckit the peas down the gramophone hole, and chokit the Caruso?' Kinnaird, the baker which was opposite the Gaiety sold delicious fruit cakes, and weddings could be held in the hall. Jakie the Barber was not only the place to go for a haircut, but you could also catch up with the latest gossip around the port. The end of a performance at the Gaiety, or the 'Gaff' as it was sometimes known, swelled the crowds already in the streets, and many may still remember that if you were a youngster you could get into the theatre for 'a penny and a red yin' - the 'red yin' being a ticket given out to children as an encouragement to go.

The theatre was often visited by University students, and occasionally they would cause something of a stir when they shouted at the players or whistled at the chorus girls. It is said that during one performance, a group of students were in the lowest box seats, and became rather unruly. A member of the audience was seen to leave his seat in the auditorium, and returned some minutes later with a bag in his hand and began to pull out eggs which he threw at the students, much to the delight of the audience.

The Kirkgate took its name from St Mary's Kirk which was built circa 1483, and which remained for many centuries as the main route from Edinburgh to the sea. It remained until the redevelopment in the 1960s when sadly, it was reduced to no more than a residential cul-de-sac.

NORTH LEITH

Until 1806, the harbour at Leith comprised that area extending from the head of Coalhill at Sheriff Brae to the ferry boat steps near to the former Sailors' Home, then situated in Dock Place. The entrance lay unprotected by piers, and incoming vessels had some difficulty in entering it due to the shifting sand bars at the mouth which caused delays due to insufficient depth of water. This led to the construction of the East and West Old Docks, the first in 1806, and the second in 1817, and the future success of the port was due to this far-sighted development.

In 1838 the control of the docks was handed over by the City of Edinburgh to the Dock Commission, and the first problem to be tackled was the deepening of the water channel at the entrance to the harbour, which had become necessary because much of the steam boat traffic had been transferred to Newhaven due

North Leith : The Quayside Mills and St Ninian's Church looking for better days

to the difficulties encountered with Leith. To attract these services back into the port, the Victoria Dock was constructed, and opened in 1852, and the East and West Piers were extended.

As a result of these developments, North Leith prospered, and from a village of only 1,000 people, it grew to a sizeable town of 30,000 inhabitants. In its earlier years, North Leith consisted of only one main street, Old Church Street, which led from the Bridgend, and continued as Sandport Street to the Short Sands, where Commercial Street now runs. From the main street, narrow closes ran down to the carpenters' yards on the river bank, where shipbuilding had been carried out for several centuries and The Ship Carpenter's Incorporation was a very important one in North Leith at that time. One of the oldest of the shipbuilding firms was Sime & Ranken, and the dry dock dating from 1720 became the repairing dock for Marr & Co. At the Old Dock gates was located the yard of Menzies, where the steamship Sirius was built, and among other firms operating during the early years were Strachan & Gavin, Morton, Cran, Hawthorn and Ramage & Ferguson. There was a period during the 1800's when Leith gave promise of becoming a great shipbuilding port, but the Clyde, and the coming of steam and iron ships drained this industry away. However, shipping trade continued to prosper, and with it the construction and opening of three further docks on the east side of the old harbour - the Albert Dock in 1869, the Edinburgh Dock in 1881, and the largest, the Imperial Dock, in 1904. These docks added to the prosperity of the area, but the community was deprived of the splendid sands which had stretched on both sides of the river.

North Leith had few attractions, and little of its history before 1439 is known, although recent archaeological excavations may uncover more information about the earliest inhabitants, and their life styles. The area once belonged to the abbots and monks of Holyrood, and at the location of what was once known as the Old Bridgend, Abbot Ballantyne built a handsome stone bridge to connect with South Leith, and he also erected a chapel dedicated to St Ninian, but when this became too small for the congregation they moved to a new church in Madeira Street in 1817.

Until the first extension of the docks, the burial ground in Coburg Street marked the limits of North Leith, and the country at that time would open onto hamlets, such as Bonnington Mills and Hillhousefield, and even Pilrig where, in the fifteenth century a peel tower once stood, and where Pilrig House was built in 1638.

MARTELLO TOWER

In order to defend the City of Edinburgh and the new docks which were being built in Leith, a Martello Tower was constructed on the Mussel Cape Rocks in 1809. The tower was based on a design used at Mortella Point in Corsica, and was built to protect against possible attack by the French during the Napoleonic Wars. It was built at a cost of £17,000, and is about eleven metres high, with walls some two metres thick, and there is evidence from inscriptions on some of the stones that Irish labour was used during building.

The Tower, or 'Tally Toor', as it was known locally, contained two barrack rooms, a store room, and powder tanks to service guns which were to be placed on top. The threat of invasion, however, never materialised, and the Tower was left to decay until 1850 when, under the direction of Lt. Col. Yule of the Royal Engineers, it was reconstructed and manned by men of the Royal Artillery from Leith Fort until 1869.

It has not been used since that time, and due to land reclamation over the area, the Tower is now landlocked.

© Walter Taylor

The 'Tally Toor' : The Martello Tower surrounded by the debris from the development at the docks

HOSPITAL DAY

Hospital Day in Leith was a special event, and it provided an opportunity for all members of the community to subscribe to Leith Hospital, which started as a voluntary institution, and was maintained mainly by the funds received from the public. Despite the contributions, however, these funds were not sufficient to cover costs, and every year since 1902 a Hospital Demonstration Committee had made a valuable contribution to the raising of money. In 1920, a Grand Pageant and Fancy Dress Parade was organised, which was claimed to be the biggest event ever staged in Leith to that date. The parade followed the route from Duncan Street into Easter Road, then to Iona Street, Leith Walk, Great Junction Street, Ferry Road, Craighall Road, Newhaven Main Street, Lindsay Road, Commercial Street, Bernard Street, Charlotte Street, and finished at the Links.

Hospital Day : Crawford's float ready to leave Elbe Street to join the Pageant

Up until 1920, a demonstration and sports event had been held, when substantial sums of money had been raised, and even during the First World War, a Flag Day had been held until in 1920, at the first opportunity since the war, a special effort was made to create a bigger and better occasion than ever before. Businesses and the community all responded to the call, and even the arguments raging about the amalgamation with Edinburgh took a back seat. It had been the custom for Leith people to assist with the Royal Infirmary Pageant, and now offers of help were extended by Edinburgh citizens towards Leith's Hospital Day.

Hospital Day was to be continued for many years afterwards, and after the Second World War, Lamb's House took over the organising. Changes to the route began to create difficulties, however, and a gap in the running of the Pageant continued for several years until Leith Rotary Club assumed responsibility for the running of the Pageant in the mid 1980's, which was organised in partnership with the Leith Festival on the Links.

PENNY BAP

The construction of the first dock in North Leith shifted bathers east to Seafield where there was a fine sandy beach, beyond which lay an area strewn with boulders called the 'Black Stanes', not to be confused with the Black Rocks, which are located further to the north. Local tales persisted that the 'Stanes' formed the ballast for ships from the Spanish Armada which were driven ashore at this point. However, they were natural formations, and eventually blasted, and used as aggregate for the building of the sea wall and new railway line to the docks which was being cut through at that time.

Only one of these boulders was spared, and this was the 'Penny Bap'. At one time it had been referred to as the 'Diel's Penny Brick', but it is more likely that as the stones in the area once resembled a table with bread rolls, and various utensils on top, it is likely that the largest of these became known as the 'Penny Bap'.

BE YEI CLEANE OR FOULLE?

The year 1645 was a disastrous one for Leith, when the plague carried off half the population. How it started is not quite clear, but it seems that it may have been connected with an outbreak in the North of England, which was carried northwards by the victorious Scottish Army when Newcastle was overrun. In December 1644, as a precaution, the Water Bailie was ordered to prevent any ship from Newcastle attempting to berth in Leith or Newhaven, and any master of such ship breaking this order was to be put to death. Furthermore, if any resident of Leith, Newhaven or Edinburgh received goods, or gave shelter to any person from these ships, they would be banished from the town for ever.

The plague began to affect many aspects of Edinburgh life, and even Parliament and the Court of Session moved to safer towns, but the situation in Leith quickly became much worse, and South Leith Parish Church Session acted as public health, social services and police authority, together with representatives appointed by Edinburgh Town Council to this body. It was David Aldinstone who held the office of Session-Clerk to this committee, and he recorded the events in South Leith with much detail, but unfortunately the records for North Leith have long since perished.

The first reference to the plague in Leith was made in April 1645, when a woman from the Yardheads, and two men from another part were confirmed as victims. Some weeks later, there was an outbreak in King James's Hospital which was the local poorhouse, and in June groups of 'ludges' were erected on the Links where all those who were infected and their contacts were taken. The number of cases continued to grow, and it was decided to divide South Leith into four quarters, each under the control of a quartermaster who kept records of numbers affected and deaths, and who was also responsible for the provision of food. The demand for food created severe problems, and distribution became even more difficult when the quartermasters were reluctant to visit the 'ludges' because of fear of infection. The epidemic appeared to reach its height in July, but corpses continued to be buried in the Links, and due to the shortage of men, women began to clean the area of muck and refuse. A petition was presented to Parliament appealing for help for the town and other areas affected by the plague, but although an Act was passed, there is no evidence that anything was actually provided. It was during November, after a period of stormy weather, that the epidemic appeared to be over, and work started to clean all the houses, wash and clean clothes and disinfect or destroy bedding, and ensure that personal cleanliness was carried out.

During the period of the plague, it was usual to hang a white cloth from a window when sickness had been notified, and sometimes the victim, as well as the whole family were prevented from leaving the home, which was also barricaded to prevent entry. If death had occurred, all contacts were taken to the 'ludges' together with their belongings, and these were located at Seafield, and in the area of Queen Charlotte Street and Links Place. Those who disinfected the infected houses were called foul cleaners, and they wore a uniform with a cloth St Andrew's Cross sewn onto it. The process of disinfection was carried out by burning whins, heather, straw and other material inside the houses, and this was followed by a thorough washing. The work was generally supervised by the Bailies, quartermasters and members of the Kirk Session whose duty it was to collect any money found in the house which could be used to supplement the plague funds. The disposal of the dead first took place at night, the bodies being carried on carts or sledges which carried a bell to warn bystanders. Only the bodies of noteworthy persons were buried in the churchyards in coffins, and the poor were simply wrapped in the coarse blanket on which they had died, and buried on the Links as soon as possible.

The records show that out of a population of 4,000 in South Leith, 2,421 had died, and Leith found itself deep in debt, with trade having been brought to a standstill, and it was to take many years before there was a return to better times.

DRAMAS AT SEA

During the early hours of 31st January 1980, HM Fishery Protection vessel *Switha* made her way through rough seas and gale-force winds towards her home port of Leith. She had left on the 17th January for a tour of duty in the North-West of Scotland, and was now patrolling the sprat fishing grounds of the Forth estuary, about a mile South-East of Inchkeith. Despite radio warnings that she was on the wrong side of the navigation buoy, she eventually grounded on the Herwit rock, and was badly holed, and soon the engine room and stoke holder were filled with water, and waves were breaking over the wheelhouse. South Queensferry and Anstruther lifeboats were called out, and some of the crew members were airlifted by helicopter to Rosyth, but *Switha's* skipper,

© Walter Taylor

Dramas at Sea : HM Fishery Protection Vessel Swritha shipwrecked
on the Herwit Rock

Captain David Dickson of North Berwick, and the remainder of the crew remained on board to man pumps, which had been airlifted to the stricken vessel. The task proved to be hopeless, however, and the remaining crew and pumps were airlifted to safety by helicopter. Meanwhile, a second minor drama had taken place, when the South Queensferry lifeboat developed engine trouble, and had to be assisted by the Anstruther boat.

The *Switha*, of some 574 tons had been built in 1948 by Cochrane & Sons of Selby, and had previously been named the *Earnest Holt*. She had been used as a Fishery Protection vessel since 1970, and was due to be replaced in the near future. Investigators reported that *Switha* could not be saved or salvaged, and it was decided to set charges within the vessel in order to release fuel oil. These were detonated on 7 February, and light fuel oil poured into the sea, which was heavily sprayed by tugs in order to reduce damage to wild life.

The wreck, which was left perched on the rock where she foundered, has long since broken in two by wave action, but the remains may still be seen on a good day to remind us of that local drama at sea.

The *Benmohr* was one of the Ben Line fleet, a steamship of 5,920 gross tons, built by Connell & Co. Ltd. of Glasgow, and launched in April 1928. On 5th March 1942, while on passage from Bombay to Liverpool via the Cape, she was torpedoed and sunk by German U-Boat 505, some 235 miles south-west of Freetown, and the crew of 56 took to the lifeboats. No warning of the attack had been given, and the three lifeboats which had been launched were soon lashed together so that they would not separate during the night. Some of the men had been wounded, but none were missing, and much praise was given to the Bo'sun, Christopher Christie of Shetland, who assisted several of the crew into the boats. The following day a plane was spotted in the distance, and soon the crew could see that it was an RAF flying boat which had responded to an SOS which had been sent just before the *Benmohr* had been abandoned. The Sunderland circled around the lifeboats, and on a calm sea made a landing, and taxied right up to the boats. At first, it was thought that only the wounded would be taken off, but the RAF captain said that he was going to take everyone, so that all 56 members of the crew, plus 11 on the Sunderland took off with its heavy load, and two and a half hours later landed safely. Radio Officer Herbert Owens of Goole in Yorkshire was given special mention, as it was his call which had brought the Sunderland to their aid, despite the fact that the radio cabin was flooding. The *Benmohr* was skippered by Captain David Anderson, and the third engineer was W Liston of Newhaven.

ROYAL ARMS

Built into the walls of the vestibule at the West entrance to South Leith Church you will find two inscribed stones which are of particular relevance to Leith. One stone is engraved with the Arms of Mary of Loraine, who was mother to Mary, Queen of Scots, and depicts the Arms of the House of Guise, quartered with those of Scotland, and bearing the inscription 'Maria de Loraine Regina Scotie 1560'. The stone is believed to have come from a house in Rotten Row, now Water Street, which Mary of Guise had reportedly kept to provide a refuge for herself, if this had become necessary.

The second stone bears the inscription 'In Defens 1565', and shows the Royal Arms of Scotland. This stone was once located in front of the Old Tolbooth, from which the Tolbooth Wynd was named.

Provost James Reoch is said to have been responsible for saving these stones, which were stored in a warehouse in Bernard Street, and about to be broken up when the Leith antiquarian Dr. Robertson discovered them, and removed them to his house in Albany Street, where they were built into a Gothic window which had been rescued from the Church during alterations made in 1836.

*The Royal Arms : The Armorial Bearings of Maria de Loraine,
1560 and Mary, Queen of Scots, 1565*

THE FINAL LAUNCH

On 15th September 1983 the sealink ferry *St Helen* slipped quietly into the water at Victoria Shipyards. She had been built by Henry Robb Ltd., and this final launching was to signal the end of shipbuilding in Leith after more than five hundred years. Henry Robb had started as yard manager for Ramage & Ferguson before the First World War, but in 1918 he decided to undertake ship repair work under his own name, and his yard quickly became known for the quality of the work done. In 1924 an opportunity presented itself to take over the yard occupied by Hawthorns, and two years later Cran & Somerville was also taken over. Finally, in 1933, his old firm of Ramage & Ferguson ceased trading, and Henry Robb Ltd. effectively gained full control of the Victoria Shipyards.

The firm now found itself in a position to design and fabricate passenger and cargo vessels, and specialise in the building of tugs, many of which gave good service during peace and war. During the Second World War, Henry Robb Ltd. built 42 ships for the British and other Admiralties, and also 14 merchant ships, as well as carrying out repairs and refitting of some 3,000 other vessels. The yard was involved in the building of Flower Class corvettes at the start of the war, and later built Castle Class corvettes, as well as 12 frigates. Several minesweepers, trawlers and recovery tugs were also built, and there was little respite for the people of Leith, with the constant noise of rivetters at work ringing through the streets.

The Final Launch : The empty slipway at the Victoria Shipyard signals the end of shipbuilding in Leith after five hundred years

The Victoria Shipyards were honoured with a visit from the King and Queen in July 1943, but later that year, launchings of a different kind were to take place, with a project that came to be known as Mulberry, and which began the build up to the D-Day landings in June 1944. A special yard was constructed, complete with all the necessary equipment, and in January 1944 the first of thirteen pier heads was launched, and then towed round to Newhaven where it was completed. The yard also built pontoons for the floating harbour, and some

600 men involved in all trades worked night and day to achieve the completion targets which had been set.

After the war, the yard continued to modernise, and orders were obtained from several shipping lines, but changes in shipping practices and raw materials saw the Port face yet another crisis, and in 1968, Henry Robb Ltd. merged with a Dundee yard to form Robb Caledon, and in 1977 they became part of British Shipbuilders. In 1982, the yard reverted to its former name, but the end was near, and after the launch of the *St Helen*, the order book was empty, and closure became inevitable.

HIGH DIVER

In April 1897 a man called Tommy Burns, described as the world's champion high diver, tested his skills in the Water of Leith. With a loud shout of '*Here goes, boys,*' he dived sixty feet from a house in Ballantyne Road into four feet of water at Junction Bridge. Luck wasn't with him on that day, however, as the ever vigilant Leith Police apprehended him, and took him to the cells in Constitution Street. He was wearing a policeman's helmet, jacket and tights, and was fined seven pounds ten shillings, or 42 days for his effort. He had dived from the Forth Bridge in 1896, but in July 1897 he died after diving one hundred feet from the pier at Rhyl when unfit.

THE SAPPER AND THE POET

Memories of the First World War still recall the horrors and heroism of the many who served in the trenches in France during that time, and the local newspapers listed their agonising columns of those who had been killed and injured. These papers also wrote of the heroism of Leith men in battle, and among those was Sapper Adam Archibald, who became Leith's first holder of the Victoria Cross, and who, in a curious way was to cross the path of Wilfred Owen, the war poet, although they were never destined to meet.

Adam Archibald was born into a Leith family in 1879, and while at Leith Walk School, did well enough to become apprenticed to a Leith plastering firm in his teens, before taking employment with Stuart's Granolithic at Gorgie, and furthering his education at technical school where he obtained several trade certificates. In 1902 he married Margaret Sinclair, and before the outbreak of the First World War they had raised four of a family. He was a keen junior footballer, and played trials for St Bernards. He was also a member of Eastfield Bowling Club, and an enthusiastic amateur gardener, who was often seen with his displays at the annual Leith Flower Show, but in 1916 Adam enlisted in the army, and eventually went to France with 218 Field Company Royal Engineers.

Wilfred Owen, was born in Oswestry in 1893, and was educated at Birkenhead Institute, and then at Shrewsbury Technical College and for a short period he became lay assistant to a vicar at Dunsden near Reading. In 1914, he went to France to teach English in a Berlitz School, but because of the war he returned to England and joined the Artists' Rifles in London, which was a training unit for potential officers. He was commissioned into the Manchester Regiment in 1916, and soon found himself in France in the trenches, but in May 1917, he returned to England suffering from shell shock, and was eventually transferred to Craiglockhart Hospital at Colinton under the care of Captain Rivers, who had developed new techniques for the treatment of neurasthenia. Owen met the poet Siegfried Sassoon at Craiglockhart, and they

Sapper Adam Archibald, VC

became good friends, and with his help he wrote some of his best poetry during this period. He was discharged from hospital during June 1918, and after a spell with a home unit he returned to France in August, and was later recommended for the Military Cross for his part in the capture of a German machine gun post.

In October 1918 the end of the war was in sight, and there was an increasing optimism that all would soon be over, but Field Marshall Haig ordered one final offensive in order to cut the German supply lines in an attempt to avoid any further delays over the signing of the peace treaty. The line chosen for the assault was the Sambre Canal on the River Oise in North-East France, and in the early hours of 4th November British artillery began to shell enemy positions across the canal. Near to the village of Ors, the 2nd Manchester Regiment, supported by 218 Field Company, Royal Engineers, prepared to make a crossing over the canal, and at the appointed hour the Sappers began their task of constructing two pontoon bridges across the canal, which was about 35-50 feet wide at the point of assault. Almost immediately, they were met with a hail of German machine-gun and rifle fire, but Sapper Archibald and the officer in charge of the bridge-building party, Major Waters, managed to escape death or wounding. They continued with their work despite the enemy fire, and eventually formed one bridgehead on the opposite bank, but only two platoons of infantry had crossed before it was destroyed by artillery. For their courage and perseverance against persistent enemy fire, often at point blank range, Sapper Archibald and Major Waters were both awarded the Victoria Cross. As a withdrawal was made to a defensive position in order to regroup, many men of the Manchesters were left dead on the canal bank, and among them was Lieutenant Wilfred Owen, who was later buried in the communal cemetery at Ors, together with many of his men who died in this brief action, only seven days before the end of the war.

Sapper Adam Archibald, VC., came home to Leith to a huge welcome, and he was to continue his life in his own quiet way until his death in 1957 at the age of seventy-eight. His Victoria Cross was presented to the Royal Engineers Museum at Chatham, and is now displayed alongside that of Major Waters, together with their citations.

P S SIRIUS

The idea of using a steam engine to power a ship had been the dream of many an engineer, but early engines had exposed the dangers of fire and explosion while at sea. A major change took place, however, with the development of Samuel Hall's marine engine, which used fresh water, and could recycle the steam back into water by means of condensers. The engine was patented in 1834, and these condensers made possible the thought that large ships driven by these engines could cross the Atlantic on a regular basis. Sailing ships had, of course, been making the crossing for centuries, but they depended on the wind and tides, and the average for the East to West crossing was around 34 days. Small steamers had crossed the Atlantic too, but these had not steamed continuously, and having to use salt water for their boilers at that time, had to make frequent stops in order to clean out salt deposits.

The *Royal William* was a Canadian ship, and she managed to keep her engines going for the full crossing, but had to shut these down for twenty-four hours every fourth day in order to clean out the salt from the boilers. The introduction of Samuel Hall's patent condenser engines was about to change the face of steam ships, and the race was on to provide regular passenger services across the Atlantic on a commercial basis.

The scene had now been set for an early East to West crosssing of the Atlantic, and two prominent figures had set their eyes on this honour. One was Junius Smith, an American businessman, who considered that a regular crossing could be made in fifteen days, and that four steamers could replace the existing service presently being provided by twelve sailing packets. The other figure was Isambard Kingdom Brunel, whose *Great Western* had already been launched at Bristol, and which was already being hailed as the 'Queen of the Atlantic'. She was already being prepared for the crossing, and was undergoing sea trials,

Sirius : A model of the P S Sirius as displayed in the British Science Museum

123

but with the winter months approaching, a decision was made to postpone the crossing until the Spring of 1838.

The British and American Steam Navigation Company had already contracted the building of the Victoria, later to be renamed the *British Queen*, but completion had been delayed and the challenge to the Great Western's crossing seemed doomed, when an approach was made to the St George Steam Packet Company to charter the steamship *Sirius*, and preparations for the historic crossing began.

Sirius was built in the yard of Robert Menzies & Son of Leith, at a cost of £27,000. She was built of wood, and her engines were built by J Wingate & Co. of Glasgow. She was also fitted with Hall's condensers, so she was best prepared for the voyage which confronted her. She was described as a sturdy little vessel, and had a length of 178 feet, a breadth of 26 feet, and the depth of her hold was 18 feet. She was schooner rigged, had a gross tonnage of 703, and her engines, rated at 320 horse power could give her a speed of 9 knots. Her normal run had been from Cork to London, and it was from Cork to New York that she would sail.

Meanwhile, the *Great Western* had suffered a setback in her preparations. While steaming to Bristol to commence her crossing, fire broke out, and she was run aground on a sandbank as a safety measure. The vessel was soon refloated, but Brunel himself was badly hurt in the accident, and missed the eventual departure of his ship for the New World. When she eventually sailed for New York, she carried only seven passengers, whereas *Sirius* carried a total of forty passengers. Provisions were picked up at Cork, and when all was ready, *Sirius* departed at 10am on 4th April 1838. She was under the command of Captain Richard Roberts RN, a native of Cork, who therefore became the Captain of the first ship to steam across the Atlantic to New York using this new found power, paving the way for regular commercial crossings between the Old and New worlds.

Without radio or any other means of communication, news of the progress of *Sirius* could only be conveyed from incoming sailing ships, and early reports were of heavy seas and strong winds, and there was a time, it seems, when some of the passengers and crew wanted to turn back, but she pressed on, and on 22nd April under a light breeze and blue skies, she slowed engines, fired signals for the pilot, and anchored off the Battery.

She had steamed a distance of 2,897 nautical miles, and although her sails had been set, it was her engines which had stood the test, and had held her course steadily for the New World. Her supplies of coal had been exhausted, but she had not had recourse to the emergency supplies held in Halifax.

New York had been taken by surprise at the arrival of the steamer from Cork, but despite grounding in the shallows off Sandy Hook, she soon lay at her berth in New York. Further excitement was to come shortly after her arrival as the *Great Western* was sighted, having escaped the worst of the Atlantic weather and made good time, but only to find *Sirius* lying at berth, and receiving all of the glory of the first East to West crossing by a passenger steamship. After all the celebrations, *Sirius* was soon at sea again, and on 18th May, she steamed into Falmouth where she delivered mail. She made only one further crossing of the Atlantic in each direction before returning to her coastal work, operating between Scotland, England and Ireland, but she was also sailed on a trial route between London and St Petersburg.

On 18th January 1847, a Cork newspaper reported that a ship owned by the Cork Steam Ship Company had run onto rocks at Ballycotton Bay, and had become a total wreck. The ship was reported to have been the *Sirius*, and many lives were reported lost in heavy seas and fog.

As part of maritime history, *Sirius* is celebrated as having been the first passenger carrying steamship to have crossed the Atlantic non stop in both directions, and this was due in no small part to the shipbuilding skills of Leith people who had built her in the yard of Menzies & Company, located just to the north of the former Custom House.

FIRST NEWSPAPER

Scotland's first newspaper Mercurius Scoticus was published in 1651, and although no mention is made of the printer or where it was printed, it is thought that it was produced in Leith. It was a weekly publication running to eight pages and contained news which was obtained from London. Within a year, this paper had given way to a newspaper which was published in London but reprinted in Leith, and this was followed shortly afterwards by the Mercurius Politicus, which was printed in Leith for Scottish consumption until 1655, when it was reprinted in Edinburgh.

WHAT'S IN A NAME?

Leith has many curious names associated with its streets, and a number of these are still retained and require explanation.

Coalhill for instance is the name given to the area bounded by the river, Henderson Street, and the old Parliament Street, and the name dates back to the beginning of the seventeenth century. However, it has nothing to do with coal, and more probably refers to the fact that the ground over this area was raised above the level of The Shore, and takes its name from the old Scots word 'cole' meaning a heap.

Little London is a name which has now disappeared from the local street maps, but the name was evident from the Petworth Map depicting the locations during the Siege of Leith in 1560. There is nothing to suggest that the name might have anything to do with London itself, but is more likely to refer to an area of open space which was once located in the vicinity of Constitution Street, Bernard Street and Maritime Street. The name might derive from the Gaelic word 'lunndan' meaning a marshy spot, and it is possible that part of the river drained through this area.

Vinegar Close was a name which appeared during the early nineteenth century, but which disappeared with the development of Henderson Street during the 1880s. It was named after the vinegar works which were located in the area.

Parliament Close can be located on Kirkwood's map of 1817, and may have had some reference to the Council Chamber located on the Coalhill which was used by Mary of Guise for her meetings of the Privy Council as early as 1555. The **Close** and the **Square** disappeared after the development of Parliament Street in 1892.

Sheriff Brae is sometimes referred to as **Shirra Brae** but who was the Sheriff? He was of course Sir James Logan of Craighouse who had a house in the area, and who became Sheriff of Edinburgh. The house was demolished in 1840 to make way for the former St Thomas' Church, which still stands and is now used as a mosque.

A **dub** was often the word used to describe a small pool of water and a 'raw' was an early word which was used to describe a row. The **Dub Raw** was a row of houses to be found in a side street leading from the Kirkgate, and probably set on wet ground where pools of water formed. It was later renamed as **St Andrews Street**, but for some time afterwards it continued to be referred to as the **Dub Raws**.

A local merchant called James Whyte built two houses in Salamander Street which he used as salt water baths. These were referred to as the **Frithfield Baths**, and were still shown on the Ordnance Survey map of 1877.

Ratoun Raw was recorded as early as the fifteenth century, and was later to be known as **Rotten Row**. It could have derived from the old French word 'raton' a rat which could have described a row of rat infested houses, but it seems more likely to have derived from an early Scots word meaning soft or friable, which would lead us to suppose that we had a row of houses built on somewhat yielding ground. It was later referred to as **Water Lane** in recognition of the water supply service which had been fed to **The Pipes** in Tolbooth Wynd, and in 1872 it was again renamed, this time as **Water Street**.

The Pipes is shown on Wood's map of 1777, and refers to the water reservoir which was located at the foot of the Tolbooth Wynd at the junction with Water Street. This was part of the improved water supply service which was brought into Leith under an Act of Parliament.

One of the strangest names connected with Leith is **Laugh-at-Leith**, which apparently referred to Coatfield Mains, and was probably a local name for a small stream which drained through the Links, and was sometimes seen and sometimes not, according to the conditions at the time.

Another strange name is **The Quilts** which referred to the location of a skittle alley which is said to have stood on the site. It was described as a park in the area of **King Street** and the **Yardheads** but this may at one time have extended over most of the area of the new housing development, and on the edge of the historic site known as **Leith Mills**.

THE CO-OP

On the 5th April 1878 a small group of people met in the Lower Assembly Hall in Constitution Street. There were about thirty people present, and they agreed that a Co-operative Retail Society should be formed. After further discussion on the matter, it was also decided that it should be called the Leith Provident Co-operative Society. Shares at £1 each were offered, and a small single-windowed shop at 147 Great Junction Street was rented in order to start the business off. It was later agreed that the Leith Co-operative should become a member of the Scottish Co-operative Wholesale Society in Glasgow.

On 27th May 1878, the shop in Great Junction Street was opened, and a year later a small bakehouse with one oven was rented at the Foot of Leith Walk. A big boost came in 1880 when the Wholesale Society opened its lavish new premises overlooking the Links, and soon the membership of the local Co-op had grown to over 400. The next major step was the purchase of the old Smith's Glass Foundry in Bangor Road to house the head office, and the local Society went from strength to strength.

There seemed to be a shop in every street, and with over 100 units in operation, it seemed that the early difficult years had been overcome. Now on a firm financial basis, shops were opened in Restalrig, Lochend, Granton, Goldenacre, Newhaven and even further afield in Crewe Road and the Boswalls. The emporium in Great Junction Street became the superstore of its day, and the inscribed panels commemorating the opening in 1911 can still be seen.

After the Second World War, the Society made significant advances in food hygiene and food handling, and the dairy in Duncan Place was completely rebuilt. At one stage, about 35,000 gallons of milk were being processed there each week. On the 75th anniversary of the Society in Leith, in 1953, a special dividend of two and sixpence in the pound was declared, in addition to the normal one and sevenpence. Pensioners received a special gift voucher to the value of fifteen shillings, and television sets were also installed in nurses' common rooms, and in convalescent homes run by the Society. In February 1968, the spacious new premises in Great Junction Street/Cable's Wynd were opened on a site known locally as the 'island site,' which had been purchased by the Society in 1936.

However, the much-needed housing was not being built quickly enough, many families were being rehoused in other areas, and these losses were to have a significant impact on the future of the Society in Leith. Local shops began to close, supermarkets began to draw shoppers away from the streets, and the co-operative movement began to decline. Now, after more than a century of service to the community of Leith, the death knell had sounded, and with the demolition of the superstore in Great Junction Street, and the building of new flats on the site, all that remains is the memory of that 'divi' number which meant so much to people when times were hard.

LEITH TOWN HALL AND LIBRARY

The official opening of Leith Town Hall and Library in Ferry Road took place in July 1932, and was considered to be one of the most important events of the day. The buildings were erected as part of the amalgamation agreement reached with Edinburgh in 1920, when the Corporation undertook to provide library and reading room facilities in Leith, and to build and maintain the halls for public meetings and other purposes.

Several suitable sites were considered, but the Town Council eventually agreed to purchase the open ground where the former manse of North Leith had stood, and which was then unoccupied. Plans for the buildings were received from Architects in Scotland and England, and were considered by Sir George Washington Browne as assessor, and the work was awarded to the firm of Bradshaw, Gass and Hope of Bolton, who also operated from an office in Constitution Street during the reconstruction of the buildings in the 1950s.

The architecture of the buildings has been described as in classical style, yet modern in treatment, and was free from unnecessary ornamentation. The Library was of simple design, with the main entrance entering from Ferry Road, and this building contained the Home Reading Room with its 26 exterior windows facing south. Furnishings were made from Japanese Oak, and were all constructed by Edinburgh craftsmen. A Reference Room and News Reading Room were also provided. To the rear, the Large Hall was approached by a private driveway from Ferry Road, and this could accommodate 1,672 people using tip-up seating, and there was provision for the installation of projection equipment. The smaller Hall had its own separate entrance, and could accommodate 490 people, and a special feature of this area was its dance floor of narrow maple strips, set on springs which could be locked and made into a rigid floor for purposes other than dancing.

The opening ceremony was held in the Large Hall before a capacity audience, and was under the Chairmanship of Treasurer Lindsay Gumley who described the event as 'a Leith day.' Lord Provost Sir Thomas Whitson, his Magistrates and City officers were dressed in their robes of office, and the platform party included Mr Ernest Brown, MP for Leith and ex-Provost John Lindsay who was Leith's last Provost before the amalgamation. After the National Anthem, the Rev Dr Donald Davidson of South Leith Church gave the dedicatory prayer, and Treasurer Gumley then invited Lord Provost Whitson to declare the Hall and Library open. Apparently, the Leith Coat of Arms had not previously formed part of the decor planned for the Hall, but as this omission had been remedied, Treasurer Gumley took some delight in noting that the addition could now be seen to be 'supporting Edinburgh as Leith had been doing for some considerable time.' In his speech, Lord Provost Whitson said that it was only a year ago that he had opened the new Leith Academy in South Leith, which was one of the finest schools to be seen anywhere and now, here in North Leith, these new public buildings had been built which he hoped would not become mere ornaments to the locality, but would become centres of service, and of benefit to the citizens. Leith's MP Mr Ernest Brown thanked the Lord Provost and the

Corporation for keeping their promise to Leith, and reminded him of the part which Leith had played in the development of the Town. After a suitable vote of thanks by Bailie Wilson McLaren, the buildings were inspected by the invited guests.

That evening, an opening concert was held in the Large Hall to a programme provided by Mr Robert Burnett's Choir and several eminent artistes, but despite the fact that the concert was held in aid of Leith Hospital, the attendance was described as meagre.

Sadly, on the night of 7th April 1941, a landmine dropped on the buildings during an air raid causing severe damage, and it was to be a further eighteen years before the reopening of the Library and Halls by Lord Provost John Greig Dunbar on 23 June 1961.

WEIRD GOINGS ON

The street which ran between Constitution Street and the old Kirkgate was called Laurie Street, and the North side of the street was once occupied by run-down tenement buildings, which local tradition said had once been used by Cromwell's troops in the 1650s. The yards to the rear of these buildings were also said to have been used as stables for horses at the time. A local feature was said to have been an ash tree which grew to a height of over fifty feet, and was fully-grown when a firm which occupied one of the yards was established around 1850. Once a mansion house had occupied the site, and in the early hours one morning, the neighbours were awakened by the collapse of the house. The owner and his son were taken alive from the rubble, but his wife lay dead. Some time later, before he died, Mr Oliphant, the owner of the mansion told the strange tale of how he and his wife had dreamed of buried treasure under the house, and how they had sold up everything in Ayr to come to Leith in search of the treasure. Unfortunately, his excavations had undermined the foundations of the house, and had buried him and his wife in the rubble.

LEITH VICTORIA BATHS

One of the finest recreational facilities provided in Leith over the past one hundred years must surely be Leith Victoria Baths, which were formally opened by Provost Bennet in July 1899. Built of polished red sandstone, the external appearance recognised its public importance, and to take advantage of the new building, a Registrar's Office was built adjoining.

The original pool was seventy-five feet long by thirty-five feet wide, and tapered from seven feet deep to three feet at the shallow end. Some sixty dressing cubicles flanked the sides of the pool, and a gallery gave spectator facilities at the upper level. Tiles, terra cotta bricks and pine finishings provided the main internal linings, and the general appearance was said to be light and pleasing. Constant warm water was provided by means of a calorifier, and the pool was kept at a constant temperature of seventy degrees, and all other accommodation at 65 degrees. If required, the water from the pool could be run off, and the void floored over to provide a substantial public hall for concerts, meetings, or for other purposes. The baths cost twelve thousand pounds to build, and all but the heating works were carried out by Leith contractors. The bronze and marble plaques just inside the main entrance commemorate the laying of the memorial stone and the construction, and list the names of the Provost, the Magistrates and Council Members. The Architect was George Simpson, who was also responsible for the memorial fountain in Starbank Park.

Engraved Stone : Coat of Arms over entrance doors

Once a few pence would have gained you entrance to the Baths, and after pushing through the heavy glazed doors you would have glimpsed your first sight of the pool with its chute, springboard, diving steps and rings suspended from roof beams by which it was possible to swing from one end to the other without getting wet! Halfway down the right side, there was an opening from which clouds of steam emerged and there, crowded together, sat the bathers in shallow warm water. The purpose of this was to wash before entering the main pool, and use it as a foot bath when leaving it. It was known as 'the hotties', and the refilling and emptying of the tank was supervised by a bath attendant.

The Leith Boys' Brigade encouraged all boys to swim and to take part in the competitions, and the Goalen Cup, which was open to all Companies attracted keen competition and some fine performances. A highlight among the swimming clubs was the Christmas Handicaps, which were strictly for amateurs, with prizes consisting only of festive foods, but no money! Many swimming galas were held which were organised by Leith Clubs, and if you had a pond-side ticket you would be provided with a towel to protect you from the splashes of divers, and from water polo matches.

Many Leith families started their swimming at Leith Victoria Baths, several of whom went on to gain the highest honours in Swimming, Diving, Lifesaving and Water Polo, and others went on to hold the highest posts in the adminstration of the sport, including the Presidency of the Scottish Amateur Swimming Association.

CAPTAIN JAMES WEDDELL - ANTARCTIC EXPLORER

Towards the middle of the eighteenth century, shipbuilding in Leith was dominated by James Sime, who had acquired much property in North Leith, and had access to quaysides for his shipbuilding business. He also petitioned for the construction of Leith's first dry dock, which lay just to the South of the present Cooperage building. After his death, his son took over the various yards and dry docks which had been left to him, and by all accounts he continued to prosper until his death in 1796, when trustees were appointed to dispose of his assets. Two of the late John Sime's foremen were named Strachan and Gavin, and they managed to obtain the lease of the dry dock, and from there continued in business until 1807, when they moved further upstream to a new yard which lay below the present bridge at Great Junction Street. It was from the yard of Gavin & Strachan that James Weddell was to begin the story of his historic voyage to the Antarctic, and have the Weddell Sea named after him.

James Weddell : The Jane and the Beaufoy in Antarctic waters in 1823

There were no doubts regarding Weddell's ability, and when he began to make a name for himself as a navigator, he was introduced to James Strachan, the shipbuilder, of St Andrews Street, Leith, and he persuaded James and his partners in the firm of Strachan & Gavin to fit out the brig *Jane* of 160 tons for sealing. He set sail south, visited the South Shetlands, and may have discovered the South Orkneys. He also met with some ships in Port Egmond Harbour in the Falkland Islands, and he returned home to the Thames in 1821 bringing news of the ships he had met there, and an account of conditions in the southern waters.

The voyage, however, was not a success financially, but once again Weddell persuaded his friend Strachan in Leith to refit the ship *Jane*, and also purchase a smaller ship called the *Beaufoy*. He set sail from the Downs in September

1822 in search of fur seals, visiting the Falkland Islands, Cape Horn, the South Shetlands, South Georgia and the South Orkneys. He pushed ever southwards, still finding open water, and reached the highest latitude ever recorded at that date. The sea was still perfectly clear of field ice, but with a favourable wind, he decided to head for home, and landed in July 1924. A copper seal of the *Jane* and the *Beaufoy* which commemorates the voyage, is now held by the National Maritime Museum.

Weddell's last voyage appears to have been aboard the *Eliza* in 1832, and he died in lodgings in the Strand on 9 September 1834, aged forty-seven. He was buried in the churchyard of St Clement Danes, and an announcement to that effect was reported in the Edinburgh Evening Courant.

Weddell may have spent some time in Leith during his friendship with Mr Strachan, and for a time in 1824 he lived at an address at 8 South Hanover Street in Edinburgh. James Weddell was not a Leither, but it was through his connection with the shipbuilding yard of Strachan & Gavin that he was given the opportunity to explore the Antarctic. He was an outstanding seaman and fearless officer, and Leith can only acknowledge the part played by him in exploring the waters of the South Atlantic, but without the assistance of Mr Strachan, his partners, and the yard of Strachan & Gavin he may never have been able to make the voyage at all.

'SIR, ARE YOU MY FATHER?'

The Straits of Dover have always provided a most important seaway for shipping, and in earlier times, ships from England, Italy and Spain sailed to and from trading ports in the Baltic and the Low Countries. It also became a great attraction for pirates, and some of the most feared of these came from Leith, and one who came to prominence during the reign of James III was Andrew Wood, the fighting merchant of Leith, who has often been referred to as the 'Scottish Nelson.' He is said to have been born in Largo around 1460, but he lived for most of his life in Leith, and owned much property there, as well as two fine ships called the *Flower* and the *Yellow Carvel*.

It was after the Battle of Sauchieburn that James III was slain whilst attempting to reach the safety of Andrew Wood's ships, but a rumour had spread that he was safely aboard the *Yellow Carvel*, together with many of the wounded of the King's army who had escaped from the battle. A message was sent to Wood by the lords, asking if he had the King on board his ship, but he said that he had not, and was duly requested to attend a meeting with the Council in order to discuss the matter. Wood was suspicious of the men who had rebelled against the King, and asked that hostages be held on board his ship to ensure his safety, and after this had been agreed, he landed at Leith and presented himself to the young prince, who was to become James IV, and who was then being held captive.

The young prince had not seen his father for some time, and thinking that Wood might be, he enquired, 'Sir, are you my father?' Wood answered that he was not, but said that he was his servant, and would be faithful to his authority until he died. The lords repeatedly asked Wood if the King was aboard his ship, but realising that he was not, he was allowed to return to his ship, leaving the lords determined to put Wood to death because of the loyalty he had shown to the King. The ship captains of Leith were later summoned by the lords, and told that if any of them would engage Wood in battle, they would be provided with artillery and provisions at the prince's expense. No one came forward to take up the offer, and Captain Barton, another of Leith's famous seamen, said that there were not ten ships in Scotland that would give Wood's two ships combat, for he was well practised in war and had good men.

In the year 1511, as Sir Andrew Wood, he was put in command of the ship *Great Michael* which was built at Newhaven, and had Andrew Barton as Master Skipper, and when he grew older, he retired to his castle at Largo where he died around 1540, and was buried in Largo Church.

The formation of a Scottish Navy is somewhat obscure, but any minor references have indicated that the Port of Leith played some part in it. It was not until the reigns of James III and IV that Scotland appears to have possessed any ships built for warring purposes, but there is no doubt that Scotland had an abundance of good seamen, and enterprising merchants. Apart from Sir Andrew Wood, merchants of Leith who came to prominence under the reign of James IV included John and Robert Barton, Sir Alexander Mathieson and William Meremonth, and there is no doubt that the name of Leith was well-respected among seafarers during this time.

CRICKET ON THE LINKS

Leith Franklin Cricket Club is believed to be one of the oldest outdoor sporting clubs in Leith, and has been playing on the same cricket square for over one hundred and fifty years. The original cricket club was called the Hermitage, which was formed some time before 1850, but in 1852 some workers in Fullartons printing works in Stead's Place formed a club called Stead's Place Cricket Club, which was sometimes referred to as Fullarton's Cricket Club. At the end of the 1852 season, the members decided to open the membership to all interested in the game, and they called the club after one of the most famous printers of the 18th century, Benjamin Franklin. Not only was he a printer, but something of a scientist, and later became one of the authors of the Constitution of the United States during the War of Independence. In 1752, he invented the lightning conductor, and the centenary of that event may have led the members of the cricket club to adopt his name.

Not too much is known about the club prior to 1863, except that it was run by Thomas Murray, the manager of the printing works, who later became Secretary, and then President of the cricket club. The early fixture list was not extensive, but teams representing Captain and Vice Captain, Married and Singles, and Other Members against the Volunteers added to the list. Franklin was very successful during the early years of play, and they are recorded as having remained unbeaten at home for the first ten years. Without declaration rules, the Club was said to have fielded all afternoon during the 1867 season, whilst Dalkeith scored 322 for nine wickets. This was the highest score by opponents until 1922, when Clydesdale scored 346 for nine wickets at the Links, of which Dan Mackay scored 257 not out, one of the highest individual innings recorded in Scotland.

The bulk of the membership of the club during the 1870's was drawn from the printing works, and the Murray and Welsh families seemed to have provided three or four players each around this period. The Sinclair family also provided several players as did the Mitchells and Clunies at a later period. The record however must have been held by the Cunningham family, as nine members apparently played for the club over a period of several years. The rise of the Leith Caledonian Cricket Club during the late 1800s attracted members from the Franklin, and the Club was at its lowest point when members of the Nelson Beaufort Club joined en masse, and began to strengthen the playing membership, so much so, that in 1899, Caledonian were beaten for the first time.

*Cricket on the Links : The members of Nelson Cricket Club, Leith,
preparing for play on the Links in 1888*

Prior to 1904, when golf ceased on the Links, playing cricket could be a somewhat hazardous sport trying to avoid the golf balls, and it is recorded that on one occasion a crowd of some two thousand chased the Volunteers away when they attempted to march across the cricket square. The Club did not function during the First World War, and the square was relaid after war ended. For several years the Club went through a period of rebuilding, but by the end of the 1920s, it had once again regained its prominent position in Scottish cricket.

The Club did not close down during the Second World War, and many good cricketers played for the Club when they were posted to the Edinburgh area for duty. Among these was A L Wisden, the grand nephew of John Wisden, the Sussex and England cricketer, who later became famous for his statistical records about the game. Several centuries have been scored by Franklin players in first eleven matches, including two by Franklin's only capped player Willie Hermiston, who played against Ireland and New Zealand in 1949. During the early years on the Links, players changed in a bell tent which was erected for that purpose, but the first clubhouse was built in 1893, and was enlarged in 1929, and was eventually demolished.

Sadly, the annual Edinburgh versus Leith cricket match is no longer played, but many will remember the interest which was shown in this match, and the many enthusiastic spectators who used to encircle the boundary line.

ALL THAT JAZZ

Since the forties, Edinburgh has produced a long list of jazzmen, many of them recognised internationally, and tributes have been paid to the late Sandy Brown and Al Fairweather who, together with Stan Greig went south to London in 1954 to form the Fairweather-Brown All Stars.

Before this however, a young trumpeter from Leith called Alex Welsh had already broken into the jazz scene, had completed a successful tour of Germany, and had broadcast, and even made a television appearance. Alex, who lived in Lorne Square, was a former pupil of Broughton High School, and he had taken an early interest in jazz with his trumpet playing, and had also played as a member of Leith Silver Band. Jazz was in his soul however, and he became a part-time member of Archie Semple's Capital Jazz Band which played in the City at that time.

An office job was not for Alex, however, and he decided on a move to London in order to further his interest in jazz, but found that there were few opportunities open to him. His early enthusiasm began to wane, until a London agent advised him that the only course open to him was to form his own band, and the first Alex Welsh Band was formed. The band began to make a big impression on audiences, and one of the first important engagements was to take part in the London Festival Hall concerts, and was soon recognised as one of the best small bands in the UK. Sadly, Archie Semple died in 1974, and the first Alex Welsh Band began to break up, but like a true Leither, Alex persevered, and the band was soon reformed. For a further ten years, the Alex Welsh Band continued to tour, playing clubs and concerts all over Europe and the UK, constantly recording, and backing international artists, but in 1977, the band again began to break up, but Alex, now in poor health, continued to play his straightforward Dixieland. His long fight against his debilitating illness was lost on 25th June 1982, and his fellow jazzmen and friends packed the church to bid farewell to this talented musician from Leith.

SMITH'S TEA ROOMS

Around 1900, Messrs J Smith & Sons opened their new premises at the corner of Duke Street and Morton Street, now Academy Street, which were declared to be the largest, handsomest and best appointed rooms in the area, with basement, ground and three upper floors. Provision had been made for a dining room and tea saloon on the ground floor, and a handsome hall at first floor level was well equipped for dinners and wedding parties.

The expectation of a 'poor oot' on a Saturday afternoon wedding drew small boys from all around, and if no handful of coins were thrown, shouts of 'hard up, hard up' would follow the bride and groom as they departed.

THE PRIDE OF ERIN

There may still be Leithers who will recall having benefited from the expert tuition of Professor Charles Wood, who, in the Palace Ballroom in Constitution Street taught newcomers the intricacies of old-time dancing. Professor Wood was responsible for dances such as the Windsor Waltz, the Waverley Two Step, and his most famous, the Pride of Erin Waltz. He wasn't a Leither by birth, but he first came to Leith in 1936, and established a dance studio in Leith Walk, and later he took over the Palace Ballroom which he ran for a number of years. He became one of the world's leading old-time dancers, and even at the age of seventy-five, he won a first prize of fifty pounds at a competition in London. His partner was Miss Alice Ross, who danced with him in competitions in the United States, Canada and Australia. He was regarded as one of the last of the dancing professors, a title given to dancing instructors at the end of the last century, but in 1957, at the ripe old age of eighty, he finally decided to retire.

THE VAULTS

One of the oldest buildings in Leith, The Vaults is first referred to in 1439, when a grant was made by Patrick, Abbot of Holyroodhouse to Sir Robert Logan, Lord of Restalrig, and his heirs. Within that document the boundaries of the lands of St Leonards are defined, and one boundary is given as '*the great volut of Villiam Logane.*' The William Logan referred to as owner of The Vaults was given the lands of Coatfield by his grandfather, but there is no indication to say how old they were at that time.

The Logans stored their grain there in an area above ground, and no more suitable place could there have been as a store as it was above the highest water mark, and subject to moist air and an even temperature, naturally obtained. Who built The Vaults, and when, is likely to remain a mystery, but tradition has it that at one time they were owned by the monks of Holyrood, and were connected by underground passage to the Abbey. From a practical point of view, this does seem highly unlikely, but at one time a passage did connect The Vaults to Coatfield House in the Kirkgate, where the owners had lived for some years.

For a century and a half, the building was occupied by J G Thomson & Co., wholesale wine and spirit merchants, but there is evidence to suggest that the Thomson family carried out business there as early as 1709. The upper storeys of the building were once used as grain lofts, but from 1885, the entire building was used by the Company. On the front wall of The Vaults an inscribed stone reads: '*James Gibson Thomson and Alexander Somerville completed this building in 1785*'.

One of the interesting features of the present building is the former Sherry Room, where a fine example of seventeenth century plaster work can still be seen. The detailing of this work is repeated within some of the state rooms of Holyrood Palace, and there seems no reason to doubt that two Englishmen, John Halbert and George Dunserfield, who undertook the work at Holyrood in the 1670s, also carried out the work at The Vaults when it was under construction.

At one time, nearly all the wines imported into Scotland came into Leith, and the Sherry Room was used as an auction room, and one of the walls housed the Vintner's Stand. Until the middle of the nineteenth century, ships carrying wine docked at the Fish Quay at the foot of the Tolbooth Wynd, and as soon as the news of a cargo of wine was received, the vintners of the town gathered in the Sherry Room where the President of the Vintners Guild took up his position on the Vintner's Stand. Samples of the various wines were carried to The Vaults where they were tasted and then auctioned.

A reconstruction of the tablet of The Association of Porters, dated 1678, can be seen bedded into the external stone wall of The Vaults, and the original was at one time located in the Square Tower, Tolbooth Wynd, over the entrance to the Old Sugar House Close.

The Porters Stone : Engraved stone of the Association of Porters, 1678

FOOD FOR THOUGHT

Before the days of protection from the Welfare State, poverty and unemployment were the harsh realities of the times, and soup kitchens were all that could sustain some families during the winter months when outdoor workers could be laid off due to the weather. Some members of South Leith Church ran such a kitchen during the 1890s from premises in the Coalhill, and then from two shops in St Andrew Street. The former halls in Duke Street were also used for this purpose before the Town Council decided to build a permanent soup kitchen in the Coalhill, at the corner of Parliament Street. A Clothing Society was also run in order help those in need during the worst of the winter weather.

LEITH THISTLE GOLF CLUB

The Leith Thistle Golf Club was formed as the result of a meeting of gentlemen which was held in the Leith Golf House on 11th March 1815. Among the rules which were drafted and then adopted was one agreeing that the members' uniform should consist of '*a green coat with green velvet collar, and plated buttons inscribed with a thistle and crossed clubs.*' Another rule was that members should dress with '*nankeen,*' or '*small white clothes*' on club days. One member was reported to have been fined half a crown for playing without the proper uniform but the following year an entry in the minute book read, '*it appeared to the meeting that much inconvenience arose from the rule that whatever member appeared at a meeting without a uniform should be fined a bottle of port for the benefit of the next dinner.*' The rule was abolished unanimously.

The uniform question appeared to be given much attention and a further minute read '*it was nowhere to be found that a red waistcoat constitutes a part of the uniform of the club and therefore, no person playing without one should be fined.*' Later, an attempt was made to change the green uniform to scarlet, but this was defeated and '*a committee of taste*' was appointed to report on a proposal to change the buttons. The committee as usual could not agree to the changes, but finally, mother-of-pearl buttons were chosen.

One of the features of the club's social activities was a half yearly dinner in the clubhouse, and at one of these it was recorded that '*many excellent glees were sung, appropriate toasts given, and with the bottle circulating very briskly the company was elevated into a very merry key, and spent the evening with the greatest harmony and good humour.*' Next day, however, following the club medal competition, 18 members and six friends dined together, and between them finished three dozen bottles of wine, were threatened by the police and broke up at four o'clock on the Sunday morning. The Secretary intimated that not being present he could take no note of fines for non-attendance or other matters.

ODDS AND ENDS

It is not often that one has the opportunity to browse through the personal notes of someone who had been working in Leith 100 years ago, but this little collection of interesting items gives a fleeting glimpse of life at that time. The person who kept the notes worked in the Burgh Chamberlain's Office in Leith, and the first item noted was a programme for the Leith Corporation Employees Fourth Annual Dinner which was held in the Peacock Hotel on Friday 20th December 1901. After the dinner, a selection of pieces for the pianoforte were played, a quartet sang '*De Ole Banjo*', then followed a violin duet and a song, and the evening ended with a duologue called '*Lochiel's Warning*.' It was reported that a good night was had by all!

The Peacock Hotel appears to have been a favourite choice for functions in those days as in December 1901, the hotel provided meals for 33 persons at a Town Hall Dinner at a cost of three shillings and sixpence per head. Strangely, in the following year a charge of only three shillings per head was made for this Annual Dinner.

One of the more amusing items was a Childrens' Treat which was held in Victoria Park on 5th July 1902 to mark the Celebration of the King's Coronation. The organisers had decided that each item in the programme would be announced by means of a bugle call and pennies were distributed by the Provost. The children sang an opening hymn and after the final '*God Save the King*' everybody cheered, apart from the children themselves.

Among the several invitation cards was one for the opening of the Imperial Dock on 8th November 1904 and for Complimentary Dinners to Sir Richard Mackie, ex-Provost of Leith in 1909 and to Provost Malcolm Smith in 1917, both of which were held in the Queen's Hotel where Woolworths now stands at the Foot of Leith Walk.

Among the cuttings of the First World War which had been kept was notice of the death of Private George Mackay, youngest son of the late Inspector Mackay of Leith Police who had been employed in the Chamberlain's Office. He was educated at Trinity Academy and Moray House and had been a member of Leith Franklin Cricket Club and the Corporation Golf Club. Also retained was a cutting noting the award of the Military Cross to Temporary Captain William Russell, RAMC, of Park Road. He had been educated at George Watsons College and Edinburgh University and at the time he had been serving with the Dorset Regiment.

One final item was a report of a fire at which Leith Fire Brigade had attended and where damage of over £3,000 had been estimated. The fire had taken some time to get under control and the Leith Observer's report read, '*The Brigade was at work for sixteen years before the flames could be extinguished*.' No doubt Edinburgh Fire Brigade had a smile at that one.

SCULPTORS AND ARTISTS

Sir Eduardo Paolozzi, RA., FRIAS., D Litt (Hon.)

Born in Leith in March 1924, Paolozzi was the son of Carmela Rossi and Alfonso Paolozzi whose families came from the region of Lazio near Rome. The family owned an ice cream business in Albert Street, Leith, and at the outbreak of the Second World War he was interned and later enlisted in the Pioneer Corps. He studied at the Edinburgh College of Art, and later with the Slade School in London and began teaching at various colleges before making his name as a sculptor. In 1975, he held an exhibition at the Fruitmarket Gallery in Edinburgh. His sculpture named *Manuscript for Monte Cassino* was unveiled outside St. Mary's Cathedral, Edinburgh in 1991, and in recognition of his family's connections with Leith, the sculpture had several stones included from the demolition of Leith Central Station. In 1995, Paolozzi presented much of his studio to the National Gallery of Scotland, and in 1999, the Dean Gallery opened and erected in the foyer his figure of *Vulcan*.

Paolozzi was knighted in 1989, but after suffering from a stroke in 2000, he was unable to complete much of his outstanding work and he died in London on 22 April 2005.

Thomas Whalen, RSA

Born in Leith in October 1903, Thomas Whalen was educated at St. Thomas' School, Leith, and later worked as a bartender before becoming a shipwright. He won a scholarship to the Edinburgh College of Art as a full time student, and was the first recipient of an Andrew Grant Fellowship. During the Second World War he presented a roundel of the *burning bush* to each canteen of the Church of Scotland. In 1951, he was commissioned for a work named Mother and Child for the Festival of Britain exhibition. Perhaps the most prominent local work is his sculpture of the *Sun* which can be seen on the frontage of the Brunton Hall in Musselburgh. Thomas Whalen died on 19 February 1975.

John Duncan Fergusson, RBA

Born in Leith on 9 March 1874. Studied medicine in Edinburgh in 1894 and then turned to art. He was influenced by the Glasgow School and spent much of his time in Paris. After a spell in London, he returned to Scotland in 1939. In 1918, he had joined the navy and undertook a series of war paintings of Portsmouth Dockyard. With Cadell, Hunter, and Peploe, he became one of the four 'Scottish Colourists.' A collection of his works is held by the Perth and Kinross Council and housed in the Fergusson Gallery. He died on 30 January 1961.

George Ogilvy Reid, RSA

Born in Leith in 1851. Painted in oils and watercolour, with special interest in the Jacobite and earlier periods. In 1891, Queen Victoria commissioned him to paint the christening of the infant son of the Prince and Princess of Battenberg.

The finished work included a portrait of Queen Victoria and 30 other royal and distinguished persons. He died in 1928.

John Smart, RSA, RSW, RBA

Born in Leith. A landscape painter in oils and watercolour who was enthusiastic for all things Scottish. He wrote and sang songs, played the pipes and wore the kilt. He published *A Round of the Links : Views of Golf Greens of Scotland.* which was engraved by George Aikman in 1893 and which has become a scarce and valued book. He was also a founder Member of the Scottish Watercolour Society. John Smart died in Edinburgh on 1 June 1899.

Robert Gavin, RSA

Born in Leith 1827. A figure painter who visited New Orleans in 1865 and became known for his Moorish subjects and for his colour rich and harmonious works. He was said to be '*susceptible to the impressions of unfamiliar life and surroundings.*' He died in Newhaven in 1883.

S S EXPLORER

The Fishery Board for Scotland acquired the *Explorer* in 1921. She was then fitted out as a research vessel and commissioned the following year at a cost of £17,000. During the 1950s, the former Scottish Home Department commissioned a new ship to be built to replace the *Explorer* but retained the original name. She was built by Alexander Hall & Co.Ltd., at Aberdeen, and was launched on 21st June 1955. The vessel was 202 ft.overall, had a beam of 32 ft. and a gross tonnage of 862. In 1984, the *Explorer* was withdrawn from service and sold to James A. White of Inverkeithing for scrapping, but so impressed by the vessel's potential were the staff at the Maritime Museum in Aberdeen that the vessel was purchased complete from the shipbreakers. However, no deal could be reached for the future of the vessel, and for the next ten years she was moored off Invergordon awaiting her fate. Finally, in January 1995, Aberdeen City Council's Recreation Committee decided to scrap the *Explorer*, but to save her engine and part of the bridge for preservation.

On a grey day during 1995, the Leith registered trawler which had been saved from the scrap heap crept slowly into her mooring at the Edinburgh Dock. The once proud fishing research vessel looked barely seaworthy, but she carried the expectation of a few supporters who had sufficient faith in her to say that one day she would sail again and would be able to grace the Port whose name was proudly painted on the stern. There were many doubtful Thomases of course who thought that the task would be beyond them, but over the years, bit by bit, the work of restoration has continued, and the belief in the project has never faltered. More money was required and a spell in dry dock was necessary for repair, cleaning and painting, but not for her the razzmatazz of her Royal companion, cosily berthed in the Western Harbour, but just a tramp that was wondering about the future.

Much work is still to be done, but hopes are high that the *SS Explorer* will sail again and bring back into Leith a further reminder of the part which the Port has played in maritime history.

HIGH LIVING

Leith's post war housing programme included the building of two infamous tower blocks called Grampian House and Cairngorm House. These twenty two storey blocks formed part of the Leith Fort development which was carried out between 1957 and 1963 and were located at the northern boundary of the site overlooking Lindsay Road and the Western Harbour.

The blocks were clad with precast concrete slabs perforated with small metal windows which gave an austere appearance from the outside which was much criticised. The blocks were never free from problems and complaints from the tenants, and following a long campaign against vandalism and poor security, the District Council eventually began to move the occupiers from the 152 flats in 1991. At the time, these blocks were reported to be the tallest buildings under construction in Scotland, but their appearance was never totally accepted by local Leithers. Technically, they were described as '*architecturally uncompromising in their sculptural boldness*' and were important due to the use of modern materials and techniques. Several plans for the refurbishment of the two towers were considered, but due to the high costs involved, they were eventually demolished.

Several tower blocks have survived the sixties, however, including Kirkgate House at 18 storeys high, and the two towers at Persevere Court and The Citadel previously named Thomas Fraser Court and John Russel Court which rise to 20 storeys high.

The flatted developments built around the same time are ten storeys high and include Linksview House, Leith Fort and Cables Wynd House, which is known locally as the '*Banana Flats*' because of its plan shape.

THE CORN EXCHANGE

One of the most interesting buildings in Leith is the Corn Exchange which was built on the site of a former naval yard and adjoined the Edinburgh and Leith Gas Works in Baltic Street. The foundation stone was laid with Masonic Honours on 16 October 1860, and the building was completed in 1862 at a cost of £6,500. This elegant structure is in Plain Italian style and has a frontage of 110ft.to Baltic Street and a depth of 70ft. to Constitution Street. One of the features internally is the roof structure which comprises single span trusses with decorative iron inserts. The main entrance is surmounted by a large and imposing domed tower and running the full length of the west elevation to Constitution Street is a fine carved frieze by John Rhind representing cherubs engaged in commercial and agricultural activities.

The Exchange was used principally as a centre of commerce and as a meeting place for society, but it also served as the drill hall for the 1st Midlothian (Leith) Rifle Volunteer Corps before the Corps was located in Stead's Place near to the Foot of Leith Walk. One of the highlights associated with the Exchange building was celebrated in March 1871 when a soiree and concert were held there in order to honour the marriage of Princess Louise and the Marquis of Lorne.

The offices were once known as the Atlantic Chambers and housed Furness, Withy & Co.Ltd., who acted as Lloyd's Agents and Insurance Brokers and also superintended the local interests of the Cairn Line of steamers, dealing mainly with Canadian traffic in grain and miscellaneous cargo traffic.

LEITH AT THE CROSSROADS?

Many years have passed since the amalgamation of Leith with Edinburgh but the stories of poor housing, unemployment and poverty during this period may still linger with those who remember the twenties and thirties. Families had to suffer, and they could only hope that one day the situation would change and a bright, new Leith, with jobs, decent wages and better housing would replace the despair for the future which many would experience at that time. The finger inevitably pointed to the City Fathers sat in their Chambers 'up the toon' for failing to heed the needs of Leith, and there is probably some truth in this because the prospect of better housing and job opportunities which were expected as a result of the amalgamation never really materialised.

Before the onset of the Second World War, Leith had a population of around 80,000, and located some of the worst slum areas in the country, where families had to live in run down tenement blocks, with only their own community spirit to sustain them. Many families of course were rehoused in the first of the City housing developments outwith the Leith area, but despite the conditions in Leith, moving out of the area to most people was the last thing that they wanted to do.

The corner of Henderson Street and the Coalhill before part demolition, upgrading to restaurant and construction of shops and flats

The housing redevelopments of the 1960s and '70s were welcomed of course, but they came at a price, as under the demolition hammer went the Kirkgate and Leith Fort and all the old streets and wynds which housed the very lifeblood of the community. The choice was always going to be a difficult one, however, as Leith people wanted to be rehoused in an area where their roots lay, and this could only be achieved by building the concrete and brick towers which are with us today. Who could deny those families who were living in deplorable conditions the chance of houses with modern conveniences and a better environment? The Census figures of 1971, over fifty years since the amalgamation with Edinburgh, record that out of 16,998 occupied houses in Leith, 6157 had no bath, 852 had no internal toilet and 3158 had no piped hot water supply, but these facts are sometimes overlooked when we reminisce fondly of the days 'doon the channel.'

After the Second World War, there was an expectation of better times to come, and local politicians, Leith Chamber of Commerce, churches and community groups continually pressed for better housing and job opportunities and the position slowly began to improve. The Dock Commissioners too were alert to the changing practices in shipping trade and the inadequacies of the facilities in Leith, and in 1953, new breakwaters were completed and plans were laid for the formation of a new entrance lock and sealing dam in order to create a non-tidal impounded harbour which could accommodate the largest ships. This development was completed in 1969, but by that time, Leith Dock Commission no longer existed, as one year later the Forth Ports Authority began to administer all of their ports as a single unit, and in 1992, the docks became part of Forth Ports plc. There is no doubt that but for the construction of the new lock gates and the creation of deep water berths, the future of Leith would have been bleak indeed.

The other great problem affecting Leith was unemployment, and this was partly due to the fluctuations in trade through the Port and the gradual demise of local industries and shipbuilding. Leith also suffered from an unfortunate quirk in the conditions regarding government development grants, as the unemployment statistics for the area could not attract the grants which were available, and many firms moved out of Leith to expand and develop in other locations which were designated for grant assistance.

During 1971, the City planners began a period of consultation with the community of Leith over the future plans for the area and many questionaires were completed, meetings and an exhibition were held, and there was a great feeling within the community that at last, they were making a contribution towards Leith's future. The concerns for the area were clearly defined: the fall in population: unemployment: sub standard housing: factory closures with limited space for expansion: lack of government grants: run down schools: poor distribution of open spaces: poor road layouts: traffic congestation: lack of car parks and a poor environment.

The Leith Local Plan was eventually approved in 1974, and in general terms it aimed to stem the physical, social and economic decline of Leith by means of development, and by increasing the potential of Leith as an area for growth. The broad aim of the plan was to preserve the maritime and traditional elements, conserve buildings of historic interest and ensure that any new development was in sympathy with its surroundings. The Leith Local Plan was finally adopted in 1980, and due to continuing pressure from the community, the Scottish

Development Agency was asked to carry out a study of the area with the task of investigating problems relating to the area and assessing its potential.

This study resulted in the launching of one of the most important programmes undertaken in Leith and involved Lothian Regional Council, Edinburgh City Council and the Scottish Development Agency which, under restructuring, became Lothian and Edinburgh Enterprise Ltd. Through its offices in Bernard Street, Leith, many projects were undertaken in order to prepare the area for inward investment, small industrial units were built on derelict land, landscaping and stone cleaning were carried out and financial assistance was made available for the conversion of former warehouses. Soon, restaurants began to open on The Shore and small businesses began to occupy several of the vacant properties. The programme began to gain momentum and was extended for a further two years before ending in 1986. The good work was continued by the Leith Enterprise Trust which continued to assist small businesses, and through its Visitor Development Group, the Leith Jazz Weekends became an annual event and plaques were placed on buildings which are of historic interest to the area.

For a year or two, Leith's fortunes seemed to be at a standstill until Forth Ports plc announced the building of the new Scottish Executive at Victoria Quay, and the refurbishment of the former Leith Sailor's Home to form the Malmaison Hotel.

Queen Margaret College also acquired the former Leith Academy Secondary School in Duke Street, Leith, when the new school was relocated at Quarryholes near to the foot of Easter Road, and soon came the news that the Tall Ships would come to Leith in 1995. Forth Ports plc pressed ahead with their plans to develop former warehouses and disused land within the dock area, a new Ocean Terminal was built to complement the increased cruise liner traffic, and the former Royal Yacht Britannia was brought into Leith, refurbished and berthed in the Western Harbour where it has become a major tourist attraction. Housing and commercial development on a large scale has continued within the Port of Leith, Western Harbour and Granton Harbour and now, the forward planning of future projects will create an international Waterfront City which will provide 18,000 new homes and increase the City of Edinburgh's population by ten per cent.

This vision of the future is considered to be the largest single planned development area in the history of the City of Edinburgh and will centre around nine new waterfront villages within the Port of Leith, comprising a range of housing developments, major cultural and heritage areas, healthcare and educational facilities, all within a safe environment. New parks, seafront promenades and green space will provide a distinct character to each of the villages throughout the Port area and new names such as Maritime Quay, Leith Sands, Waterfront Plaza and Mulberry Bay will become the postal addresses of the new Edinburgh Forthside.

The scale of this vision for the future is hard to imagine, but one may question what will happen to the old town of Leith? How can it survive? The planned

New housing developments at Western Harbour

development outlined for the Port of Leith does not make any reference to the development of the town of Leith with its historic past, strong identity and community spirit. It will be necessary to sustain our churches, schools, businesses and local organisations as the regeneration of the community, old and new, is vital for the long term future.

Leith is indeed at the crossroads, and while the projected developments are welcomed, a watchful eye will require to be kept open for the decision making of the future to ensure that Leith's historic past is not forgotten.

NOTE ON SOURCES

Except where specifically acknowledged, the information included in this work is believed to be 'common knowledge' and its sources are many and varied.

Whilst there has been no verbatim use of copy, it is possible that some has been gleaned from the publications listed below and this is gratefully acknowledged.

SOURCES

Leith Observer
Edinburgh and Leith Burghs Pilot
Leith Gazette
Evening Dispatch
The Leith Porthole
Leith Burghs Pilot
Edinburgh and Leith Observer

The Life and Times of Leith
James Scott Marshall (John Donald 1985)

The Church in the Midst
James Scott Marshall (The Edina Press 1983)

Captain Roberts of the Sirius
Daphne Pochin Mould (Tower Books 1988)

The Fight Game in Scotland
Brian Donald (Mainstream 1988)

The Last Picture Shows - Edinburgh
Brendan Thomas (Moorfoot 1984)

Housing the People
Richard Rodger (City of Edinburgh Council 2000)

The Sea Dominies
Iain Crawford (Leith Nautical College 1987)

Leith-Built Ships at War
(Henry Robb Ltd)

The Short Arm of the Law
(John Long Ltd 1966)

The Streets of Edinburgh
(Edinburgh Impressions, 1984)

Port of Leith Project
(Forth Ports plc. 2005)